SCRAP
HAPPY
SEWING

retro mama

SCRAP
HAPPY SEWING

Kim Kruzich

18 easy sewing projects
for DIY gifts and toys
FROM FABRIC REMNANTS

D&C
David and Charles

www.stitchcraftcreate.co.uk

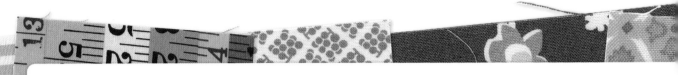

CONTENTS

INTRODUCTION

It took a number of years before I caught the sewing bug, even though I grew up watching my mom sew. Each year around Halloween, I spent hours studying her snip and stitch beautiful stacks of fabric into terrifying shark costumes for my brother and glittery princess gowns for me, but it seemed such a magical transformation that I didn't believe I could possibly learn those skills myself.

After I was married, my mom bought me a basic sewing machine using Betty Crocker points she had saved, so I could mend clothes and other things around the house. A few years later, when I had kids, I decided – in my sleep-deprived state – that I needed a creative outlet, and at Christmas time made aprons for the gals in my life. I squinted and seam-ripped and swore (*mostly* under my breath) my way through that store-bought pattern in the quiet hours of the night when my little boys were sleeping, and ended up with several aprons that I couldn't have been more proud of. I had a sense that sewing could, and should, be easier, and as I gradually taught myself how to sew, I found it simpler to devise my own patterns than to follow those designed for experienced seamstresses.

I opened a little shop online selling headbands and aprons of my own design, and continued to expand my sewing repertoire, learning to make pincushions, bags, and soft toys by trial and error. There is something immensely satisfying about collecting bits of felt and fabric and thread and stuffing, and then working, hunched over the sewing machine like a mad scientist, until you have produced an adorable stuffed animal that your bouncing baby is giving a real-life squeeze. I couldn't wait to share my patterns in my shop and on my blog so that others could have the same experience. And now, I am thrilled to be able to offer a collection of new patterns in the form of this book!

All of the projects are made or embellished with scraps, remnants, and small quantities of fabric. It didn't take long for me to accumulate lots of fabric scraps, trims, and buttons, and I bet it's the same for you! Even if you are new to sewing, you may have found it difficult to part with a favorite wool jacket too damaged to repair, or a child's soft corduroy pants, long outgrown. So dig into favorite scrap fabrics, make use of those old garments, and create something new and magical for yourself and your loved ones!

This book was written with the beginning stitcher in mind, so even if you have little sewing experience, you will find that all the patterns have step-by-step photos and thorough instructions. For beginners and those returning to sewing I have included a list of essential tools for your Basic Sewing Kit and information on fabric to help you build (or rediscover) your stash. The templates you will need and the basic techniques used are given after the project sections. At the end of the book you will find my favorite resources for fabrics and sewing notions.

My hope is that whether you are an experienced stitcher or just starting out, you will find new techniques to try, experiment with different ways to use materials, and develop your creativity by customizing and embellishing the projects to your own style. So let's dive into that scrap basket and start creating!

Kim

For Mom, Sewing Sorceress

Using This Book

- Read the project instructions all the way through before starting a project, to help you visualize it and plan ahead. This will save time – and hopefully reduce mileage on the seam ripper.

- Review the Techniques section to familiarize yourself with the methods and terminology that repeat throughout the projects. There you will find photographs and descriptions to help you learn or re-learn the skills.

- For the machine stitches and hand stitches used refer to Techniques: Machine Stitches and Techniques: Hand Stitches.

- A project's materials list will say where templates need to be used to cut the fabric pieces, so check the Templates section for the templates you will need for each project.

- Templated items in the materials list with a * next to them are to be cut at the start of a project. Those templated pieces without should be cut during the making process (as indicated in the project instructions).

- Measurements are listed in both imperial and metric units. All the projects were sewn with the imperial dimensions, so I recommend using these measurements.

- Be creative! Add your own embellishments, experiment with different trims and hand stitching, and personalize the projects to make the style just right for you or the recipient of your beautiful, handmade gift.

EQUIPMENT & MATERIALS

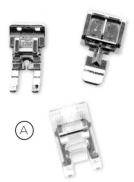

(A)

Basic Sewing Kit

Whether you are new to sewing, returning after a long hiatus, or just need a refresher, you will want to have the following tools for craft sewing.

Sewing Machine

You do not need an expensive sewing machine for craft sewing! Many inexpensive models have more than enough functions to make a ton of gorgeous projects. My favorite features to look for on a machine are: a top-load bobbin with a see-through window, multiple stitch functions including zigzag stitch and triple stitch, adjustable needle position, and a free arm for sewing circular items, such as the topstitching on a bag. If you intend to make clothes you will want your machine to have buttonhole stitches as well.

Sewing Machine Presser Feet (A)

Many machines come with basic presser feet (see photo A), though you may find that you need to purchase additional feet as you build your sewing repertoire. The following are my most used presser feet.

- A general-purpose foot for all-round sewing. I use it for piecing patchwork, triple-stitching reinforced seams on toys, and sometimes for zigzag stitching appliqués.

- A zipper foot for installing zippers. It's also useful for sewing seams very close to the edge of folded fabric.

- An appliqué foot looks similar to a general-purpose foot, but the bottom is transparent, allowing more visibility when sewing around appliqués.

- A quarter-inch foot is sized so that if you place the fabric you are sewing directly under the foot, lining it up just to the right-hand edge, your seam allowance will be exactly ¼in. You can also achieve a ¼in seam allowance with a general-purpose foot if you are able to adjust the needle position on your machine.

- A walking foot/even feed foot is designed for sewing through multiple layers of fabric, such as when quilting. It has its own set of feed dogs to help feed the fabric from the top and bottom. Use this foot any time your project has batting (wadding).

Sewing Machine Needles

All the projects in this book require 'sharps' needles (universal needles). I use 80/12 for lightweight fabrics and quilting cotton, 90/14 for slightly heavier fabrics and topstitching, and 100/16 for sewing through denim, other heavy fabrics, or many layers of fabric. I recommend changing your sewing machine needle after each project, when you begin quilting or topstitching, or if your machine starts to skip stitches, the thread tangles frequently, or the stitches become uneven.

Scissors (B)

I have a pair of large dressmaker's shears for cutting fabric, as well as small embroidery scissors for snipping threads or trimming notches into fabrics. Pinking shears (or a pinking rotary cutter) are helpful as well – they have a zigzag edge for reducing fraying when trimming seam allowances.

Quilter's Rulers (C)

These transparent, plastic rulers are essential for any patchwork or quilting project. Used with a rotary cutter and self-healing mat, you can quickly make very accurate cuts of any size. My most used ruler sizes are 3in x 18in, 6in x 24in, as well as 6in and 12½in squares. A ruler with ⅛in grid lines is helpful for precise cutting. I recommend getting a 6in x 24in ruler to start, as it is extremely versatile, and add a large square if you plan to make quilts. Store your rulers in a straight or flat position so they do not warp.

Rotary Cutter (D)

This fabric cutting tool has a rolling blade, much like a pizza cutter. I love my Olfa rotary cutters – the blades can be locked in the closed position, which is very useful for preventing accidental cuts. I use a 45mm rotary cutter for most patchwork projects, and it can also cut around large curves. A smaller 28mm rotary cutter is handy for cutting around templates with smaller curves. I keep an extra rotary cutter with a pinking blade to make trimming seam allowances easy.

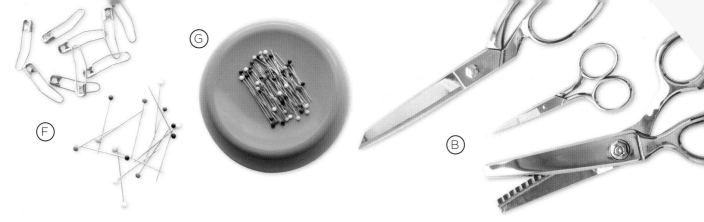

Self-Healing Mat (E)

You will need one of these mats for rotary blade cutting. Get the largest mat that will fit on the table where you will be cutting, and invest in a high quality brand such as Olfa, so you can be sure the mat is truly self-healing. Always store your mat flat so it will not warp.

Iron and Ironing Board

Buy a good iron with adjustable heat settings and spray/steam buttons. It is best to use distilled water to prevent minerals from building up in the iron. You can also get a hot-iron cleaner, which usually comes in a little tube and is a life saver if (when!) you accidentally melt fusible materials onto your iron. Read the instructions carefully to be sure you are using it safely.

Pins (F)

Start with a set of straight pins for holding pieces of fabric together. Glass-headed pins are nice as they do not melt if you accidentally touch them with your iron, but regular plastic round- or flat-headed pins are fine too, as long as you are very careful with them. If you plan to quilt you will also need quilter's safety pins for pinning your quilt sandwich. Always remove pins *before* you sew over the area that is pinned.

Magnetic Pincushion (G)

Magnetic pincushions are great for keeping straight pins handy. The pincushion 'grabs' the pins from your fingers for easier pin removal while sewing, and it also makes a good fabric weight. Store scissors and other metal tools away from the pincushion, though, as over time it can cause them to magnetize. I like to use handmade pincushions for storing threaded hand sewing needles for easy access.

Fabric Marking Pen (H)

I love air-dry fabric ink pens for tracing around patterns and marking quilt lines, but water-soluble ink works well, too. Air-dry ink fades on its own, and can last from a few minutes to several days depending on the type of fabric it is used on. Water-soluble ink can be removed with a clean, wet cloth. For dark fabrics, white fabric pencils or chalk work nicely.

Seam Ripper

This tool lets you gently cut threads when a seam goes awry. I prefer a flat handled seam ripper as it lies closer to the fabric, requiring less of an angle to use it, and it will not roll away. I typically use a seam ripper at least once on every project!

Point Turner

You can purchase a special tool for this purpose, but you probably already have items around the house that will work just as well. Chopsticks are my favorite, or use a crochet hook.

Binding Clips (I)

These are useful for holding together many layers of fabric, such as when making a bag or sewing the binding onto a quilt. Some clips look like hair barrettes (actually, hair barrettes work quite well for this purpose!), while others are pinch-open clamps with a flat side.

Hand Sewing Needles

Needles for hand embroidery are often found in a variety pack with different lengths and eye sizes. I also have larger darning needles for sewing with yarn or attaching buttons to cushions.

Thimble

I mainly use a thimble for sewing binding onto quilts, but you will also find it useful if you plan to do a lot of embroidery. Having a comfortable thimble really makes a difference in your hand sewing experience. My favorite thimble is leather with a double-sided metal tip.

Cardstock

I prefer to print small templates on cardstock so I can easily trace them onto fabric. I find my cuts to be much more accurate this way than when lifting the fabric to cut around a regular paper template. I store my templates in labeled file folders that have the sides taped.

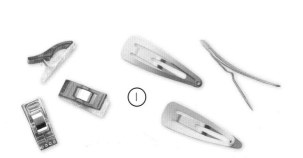

Lint Roller (J)

I love my lint roller! It is so helpful for picking up those little bits that stick to the back of your fabric before attaching fusibles, or for quickly cleaning fuzz and stray threads from your clothes or project after sewing.

Snap Fasteners (K)

A number of the projects in the book use snap fasteners. I've used three different types – sew-on, magnetic, and pearl. They are all easy to fit and are readily found online or at your local craft shop.

Fabrics and Other Materials

This section describes the fabrics and other materials that have been used for the projects in this book.

Quilting Cotton

Quilting cotton is my favorite kind of fabric to work with because it comes in an endless and ever-expanding variety of colors and prints, and is versatile for almost anything you could want to sew. Quilting cotton is considered 'mid-weight' and is a woven fabric that has very little stretch compared to knit fabric, such as cotton jersey. You can find high quality quilting cotton at your local quilt shop or online retailers that sell designer fabric. Some of my favorite online fabric shops are listed in the Resources section.

Linen and Linen/Cotton Blends

Linen fabric is made from the flax plant and has a wonderfully natural feel and look, however 100 per cent linen can be tricky to cut and sew so I don't recommend it for beginners. All the projects in this book that use 'linen' are made with linen/cotton blends, which behave a little more like quilting cotton. If you do want to sew with 100 per cent linen, you can stabilize it by attaching a lightweight fusible interfacing to the back of the fabric.

Corduroy

Cotton corduroy is just the thing for adding texture and weight to a project. It comes in a range of different 'wales', or number of bumpy 'cords' per inch. I love to use standard or narrow-wale corduroy on animal softies because it gives them an old-fashioned feel, and adds tactile interest for little ones. Corduroy is also great for making bags and is a good insulating fabric.

Thread

Cotton-coated polyester thread, or all-purpose thread, is suitable for all the projects in this book. I recommend experimenting with different brands until you find one that you prefer. The other thread I use on many projects is hand quilting thread, which is stiffer than all-purpose thread, and durable for closing stuffing holes, in addition to quilting by hand.

Batting (Wadding)

I use 100 per cent cotton batting for quilted projects. It is easy to care for and gives quilts a wonderful vintage feel. You can purchase batting for specific sized quilts (e.g., twin, double, queen, and so on) or on a roll. One twin-sized pack of batting should be enough to complete all the quilted projects in this book.

Fusible Interfacing

This is a type of interlining used to add weight and body to fabric. One side is smooth, and the other textured with a heat-activated adhesive. Never place an iron directly on fusible interfacing but always use a cotton press cloth between the interfacing and iron. I prefer to use interfacing that is at least one weight lighter than the fabric. For instance, on a mid-weight quilting cotton, I use sheer-weight or lightweight interfacing to avoid obvious creases or bubbles in the fabric.

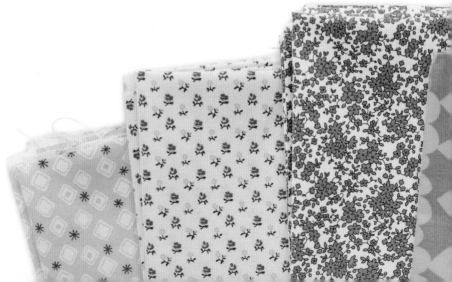

Fusible Web

This is a different type of interfacing that is used to attach one piece of fabric to another with the heat of an iron. I use it most often for appliqué projects. For instructions on how to use fusible web, see Techniques: Appliqué.

Stuffing

Although I use cotton batting (wadding) for quilted projects, I use polyester fill (also called fiberfill) for my softies and pincushions. Polyfill is less likely to irritate allergies, which is important for items unlikely to be washed often. There are many types of stuffing, however, including wool, cotton, and silky polyester, so experiment to find what you like best.

Embroidery Floss (Cotton)

Six-stranded cotton embroidery floss comes in a variety of colors, and the strands can be divided in order to sew thin or thick decorative stitches by hand. I also use embroidery floss for sewing on buttons.

Felt

The craft felt found in large hobby stores is shiny, stretchy, and made with acrylic. Instead, I recommend using wool blend (wool/rayon) or 100 per cent wool felt. It is thick, durable, and easier to sew than synthetic felt. It costs a bit more, but your results will be more beautiful and long-lasting. Wool blend felt typically consists of 20–35 per cent wool, comes in hundreds of colors, and can be found in ready supply at many online shops.

Fusible Fleece

This is a synthetic, batting- (wadding-)like material with heat-activated adhesive on one side. I like to use it to add weight and body to projects like bags.

Stabilizer

Sew-in stabilizer is sold from the bolt or in packages, and helps to add shape to projects. I find it helpful to add strength to a fabric that will be used heavily, such as fabric that has snaps.

Scraps and Remnants

Even if you are new to sewing, you probably already have a lot of fabric that you can use for projects, so raid your closets for old bed linens, linen or cotton curtains, corduroy or wool jackets or pants, cotton button-down shirts, and woven baby clothes. Flannel baby blankets are wonderful for making softies. I also love to sew with vintage bed linens. Be aware, though, that vintage linens are often polyester/cotton blends, so be very careful with the iron temperature (lower the heat setting and use a press cloth). It may be necessary to adjust your sewing machine tension as well.

If you have already sewn a few projects, you are sure to have some favorite scraps stashed away. It can be a fun challenge to use only remnants from your scrap basket to complete a project. However, if you need to build your scrap collection with new quilting cottons, a great place to start is with pre-cut fabric.

Pre-cuts come in many different sizes: 2½in (6.5cm) squares (often called mini-charm packs), 5in (12.5cm) squares (often called charm packs), 2½in x 44in (6.5cm x 112cm) strips (called jelly rolls by Moda), 10in (25.5cm) squares (called layer cakes by Moda), hexagons, and more. Typically, all of the fabrics in a particular line are included in pre-cuts – it's so easy to coordinate when all the prints already go together! Another way to add to your fabric collection is with fat quarters, which are quarter yards of fabric cut so that you have a nice-sized rectangle (18in x 22in/46cm x 56cm) to work with instead of a narrow quarter yard (9in x 44in/23cm x 112cm). You can find pre-cuts, fat eighths, and fat quarters at your local quilt shop and through many online retailers.

EQUIPMENT & MATERIALS 11

HOME SWEET HOME

Keep Tidy
SHOE MAT

When my kids come home from school they tend to leave their shoes strewn about in the entryway, but a cute patchwork mat helps keep shoes tidy and looks cute too! With embroidered initials or names, it also makes a sweet keepsake. As an alternative, you can make a mini quilt wall hanging with baby's footprints or handprints, and embroider his or her birthday and weight.

FINISHED DIMENSIONS:
Variable, depending upon the size and number of footprints used. All seam allowances are ¼in (5mm) unless otherwise stated.

From Your
Scrap Bag

(Cut fabric pieces using the relevant Templates *)

Basic tools
(see Equipment & Materials)

Assorted cotton prints
For patchwork, each 4in (10cm) high and 1¼in–2¾in (3cm–7cm) wide

As many sets of footprints as desired, each from a different print *

One cotton print for backing, approximately ½yd (0.5m)

Linen/cotton blend
Approximately 1yd (1m)

Lightweight fusible interfacing
Approximately 1yd (1m)

Cotton solid
One 2½in (6.5cm) wide bias-cut strip for binding

Fusible web
For backing footprint fabrics

Cotton batting (wadding)
Cut to size as directed in instructions

Rick rack
½in (1.3cm) wide x 3yd (3m)

All-purpose thread
For piecing, appliqué, and quilting

Black embroidery floss (cotton)

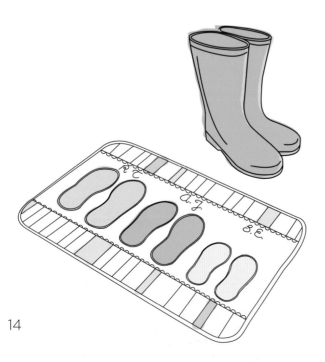

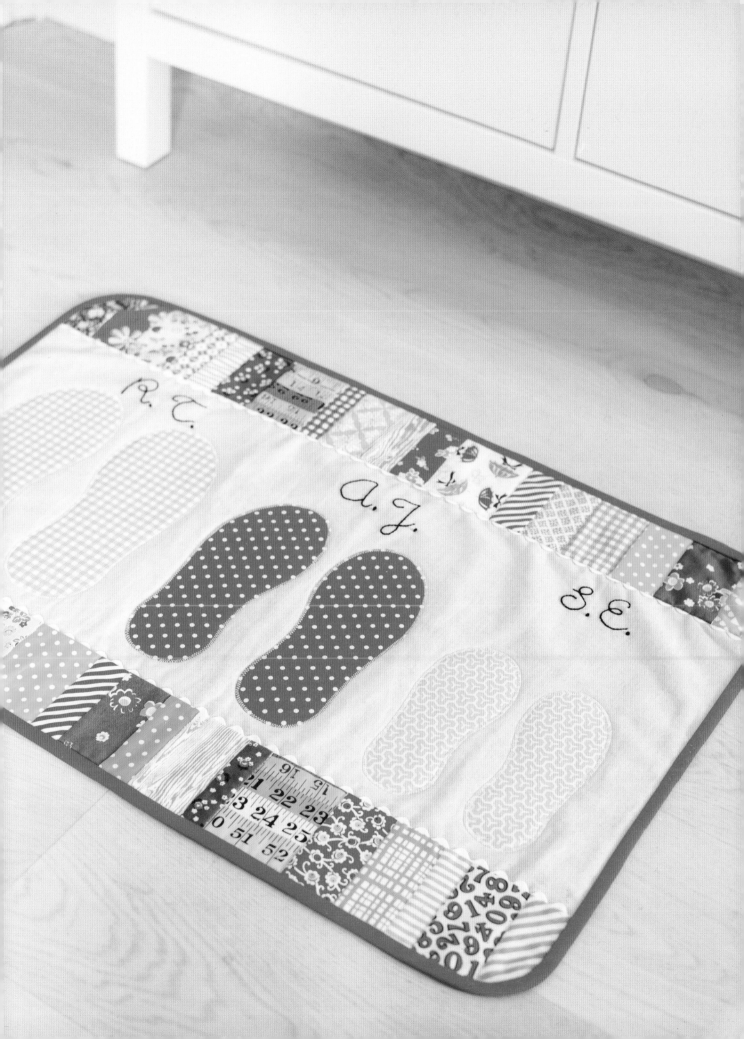

To Assemble the Mat Front

1 Back the footprint fabrics with fusible web and use the templates provided to cut out the shapes. Fuse the interfacing to the wrong side of the linen. My linen was cut at 12½in x 28½in (32cm x 72cm) but you may want different numbers of footprints. So, to determine the size of the linen you need to cut, copy the footprint templates provided in the sizes you require. To determine the width, place all the footprints on the linen, starting 2½in (6.5cm) from the left edge, with ½in (1.3cm) between footprints, 1¼in (3.2cm) between sets of footprints, and allowing 2½in (6.5cm) past the right edge of the last footprint. To determine the height, the linen should be 2½in (6.5cm) above and 1in (2.5cm) below the largest footprint.

4 Draw a line with a disappearing ink fabric pen on the front of the linen just above the footprints, for placing the embroidery. Use a light box or sunny window to trace the initials or names onto the linen with the fabric pen, centered above the footprint sets. Hand embroider the desired letters with backstitches using six strands of embroidery floss. Dot each of the periods (full stops) with French knots.

2 Once you have cut your linen to the right size, place the fabric footprints on the right side of the linen, correctly spaced, and fuse them to the linen with an iron (see Techniques: Appliqué).

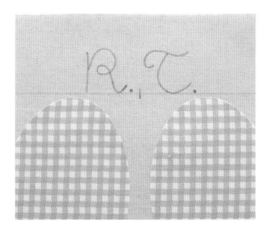

3 Print out the names or initials you want to have using the desired font and size. I used a font called Little Days Alt, at a 125 point size, which is about 1¼in (3cm) high. Your computer should have many fonts you can choose from. Draw a line down the center of the printed letters.

Keep It Simple
If using an air-drying fabric pen, press over your traced lines with an iron to make them appear darker or to reappear, even if they have already faded.

5 Place rick rack along the top and bottom edges of the linen and baste (tack) ⅛in (3mm) from the raw edges.

6 Sew the patchwork pieces long sides together so they are 4in (10cm) tall and the width of the cut piece of linen. Press seam allowances toward the darker fabric. Make one set of patchwork each for the top and bottom of the mat.

To Appliqué and Quilt

1 Cut one piece of batting (wadding) and one backing piece, each at least 8in (20cm) taller (to leave room for the patchwork) and 2in (5cm) wider than the linen piece. Place the backing fabric face down and the batting on top of the backing. Center the linen on top, right side facing up, and pin.

2 Using a machine zigzag stitch and matching thread, zigzag stitch around the edge of each footprint.

3 Smooth all the quilt sandwich layers, then pin and sew one patchwork strip to the top of the linen, raw edges and right sides together. Sew the other patchwork strip to the bottom of the linen. Press the patchwork strips open.

4 Quilt the patchwork in the ditch (in the seams), between each of the fabrics.

To Finish

1 Square up the mat and cut the width to size – I trimmed the sides to 2in (5cm) wider than the first and last footprints. Use a cup or small plate to mark and cut curved corners on the mat.

2 Press the 2½in (6.5cm) wide bias-cut strip into single-fold tape (see Techniques: Making Binding). Bind the mat with the binding using a scant ⅜in (1cm) seam allowance (see Techniques: Binding Curves). Sew the binding in place by hand or machine to finish.

Fox
CLOTHESPIN BAG

This sweet sleepy fox is an adorable helper whether she is holding clothespins outside on the line or keeping treasures in your little one's room. She features a deep front pocket, swooshy felt tail, and cute felt ears and eyelashes. Try making your fox with a brown reproduction print, vintage bed sheet or feedsack for a country feel, or make a gray fox with silver fabric and felt.

FINISHED DIMENSIONS:
18½in high x 12in wide (47cm x 30cm), including hanger. All seam allowances are ¼in (5mm) unless otherwise stated.

IMPORTANT:
Your hanger shape may differ from mine! Center your hanger on the back pattern piece – the pattern should be ¼in (5mm) larger than the neck and sides of the hanger. If it does not match, you will need to alter the back, lining, and head templates so that the dimensions are ¼in (5mm) larger than the hanger.

Additionally, when cutting fabrics, fold the fabric and place the edge of the template on the fold where indicated with arrows, then cut around the template. Do not cut along the folded edge of the fabric.

From Your
Scrap Bag

(Cut fabric pieces using the relevant Templates *)

Basic tools
(see Equipment & Materials)

Orange-brown cotton fabric
One back, one head, and one pocket piece *

Off-white cotton fabric ½yd (0.5m)
One back lining, one head lining, and one pocket lining piece *

All-purpose thread to match outer, lining, and felt colors

Orange-brown wool blend felt
One tail, and four ear pieces *

White wool blend felt
One chest, two ear centers *

Black wool blend felt
Two eyelashes, one nose *

12in (30cm) wooden, child's dress hanger

To Assemble the Head and Pocket

1 With the orange-brown back and the off-white cotton back lining pieces, press the top short curve down ¼in (5mm) toward the wrong sides. Set aside.

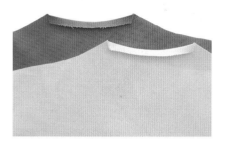

2 Place the head and head lining pieces right sides together and pin. Sew the top short curve and the long curved sides toward the nose but leave the upper curves unsewn. Trim the seam allowances.

3 Turn the head piece right side out and then press. Topstitch the three seams you stitched in Step 2 and leave the other edges unsewn.

4 Place the off-white pocket lining right side facing up, then place the skinny part of the fox head on top, orange-brown side up. Center the skinny end on the pocket.

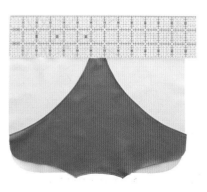

5 Next, place the front of the pocket on top of the head and pocket lining, right side facing down, matching the straight edges, and pin. Sew a seam only across the top edge with the skinny nose piece. Open up the pocket pieces so they face each other and carefully press the top edge. Topstitch the top of the pocket.

To Sew the Felt Pieces

1 Using white thread, center the chest felt on the front of the pocket, pin, and edge stitch. Place the white ear center pieces on top of two of the ear pieces. Pin and edge stitch.

2 Using orange-brown thread, stack the two ears, plus inner ear pieces onto the remaining ear pieces, pin, and edge stitch. Place the tail on the pocket piece, with the right side of the tail 2½in (6.5cm) below the top of the pocket. Pin and edge stitch.

Keep it Simple
To add a ¼in (5mm) seam allowance, tape two pencils together side by side and trace. The outer line will be ¼in (5mm) away from the original line!

3 Switch back to white thread. Place the white tail tip on the tail piece and edge stitch.

4 Using black thread, center the nose over the snout bottom and pocket, then edge stitch. Next, place the eyelash pieces on the right side of the large lining piece and zigzag stitch over the top edge. Use the head/pocket for a guide – the eyes should be about 3¾in (9.5cm) away from the center of the nose, and 3in (7.5cm) above the top of the pocket.

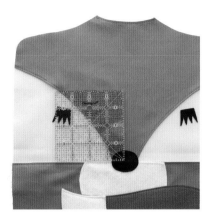

Sew Perfect

Remember to change your bobbin thread to match the color of fabric on the underside of what you are sewing. Sometimes you will have one color on top, and a different color on the bottom.

5 Place the ears white side down, with tips pointing down, on the right side of the head only, according to the pattern placement. Baste (tack) very close to the edges to hold securely in place.

To Finish

1 From bottom to top, stack the pieces as follows; back lining (white with eyelashes) right side facing up, head/pocket piece (orange-brown side) right side up, orange-brown back piece right side down.

2 Pin around the edges and triple stitch all around except the small top curve. Double check to make sure you have sewn through all the layers all the way around.

3 Trim the seam allowances around the curves. Reach through the top hole between the orange-brown layers and turn the fox right side out. Carefully press the edges.

4 Pin the two unsewn curved edges together, and topstitch. I find it easiest to sew with the lining facing up.

5 Insert the hanger under the head to finish.

Easy as Pie Apple
POTHOLDER

Bright red and green prints are even more cheerful when combined with a cotton/linen blend on this retro potholder. The stems are made with printed twill tape that doubles as a hanging loop. Layers of natural fibers – dense fabrics such as cotton twill or duck – provide excellent protection from heat when sandwiched between cotton batting (wadding), or use two layers of insulated batting instead. Pair a potholder or two with a homemade apple pie for a delicious housewarming gift!

FINISHED DIMENSIONS:
8½in high x 10½in wide (21.5cm x 26.5cm), without stem. All seam allowances are ¼in (5mm) unless otherwise stated.

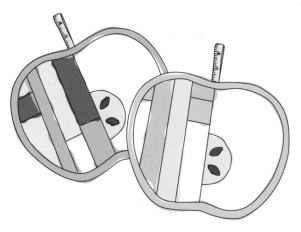

From Your
Scrap Bag

(Cut fabric pieces using the relevant Templates *)

Basic tools
(see Equipment & Materials)

Assorted cotton prints
Several red or green prints for patchwork, varying widths and lengths, at least ¾in wide x 10in high (2cm x 25.5cm)

One 2in x 34in (5cm x 86.5cm) strip of bias-cut fabric for binding

One apple center from cream print *

Two 'seeds' from black or brown prints *

Cotton/linen blend
One 10in x 6½in (25.5cm x 16.5cm) piece for front of apple

One 11in x 13in (28cm x 33cm) piece for back of apple

Lightweight fusible interfacing
One 10in x 6½in (25.5cm x 16.5cm) piece for backing linen for front of apple

Cotton twill or duck
One 10in x 12in (25.5cm x 30.5cm) piece for insulation, any color

Cotton (or insulated) batting (wadding)
Two 10in x 12in (25.5cm x 30.5cm) pieces

Fusible web
For backing apple center and seeds

Twill tape
7in (18cm) length, for hanger

All-purpose thread
For piecing, quilting, and appliqué

To Piece, Appliqué, and Quilt

1 Place the cotton/linen back piece right side down with the batting (wadding) and other insulating layers centered on top. (I placed twill between the two layers of batting.)

2 Place a cotton print strip (or pieced strip) on top of the batting (wadding), hanging over ¼in (5mm) to the *right* of the center, e.g., the right edge of the strip is 6¼in (16cm) from the left side of the batting. Place the next strip on top of the first, right sides together and matching the left edges of the fabric. Sew down the left side of the strips, through all the layers of batting and fabric. Turn over the top strip and press with an iron. Continue sewing strips until the left half of the batting is covered.

3 Apply fusible web to the back of the cream-colored print for the apple center and to the print for the seeds (see Techniques: Appliqué). Place the apple center right side facing the patchwork, lined up with the right edge of the patchwork and about 2in (5cm) above the lower edge of the batting (wadding).

4 Back the 10in x 6½in (25.5cm x 16.5cm) linen rectangle with fusible interfacing, then place it right side down on top of the apple center, with the long side lining up with the right side of the patchwork. Sew the linen along the right side. Open up the linen and press, carefully avoiding the appliqué with your iron.

5 Mark quilting lines with a disappearing ink fabric pen and quilt the linen side first. My quilt lines are ⅛in–½in (3mm–1.3cm) apart. Turn over the apple center appliqué piece, fuse it to the linen with a hot iron, then mark and quilt the patchwork side.

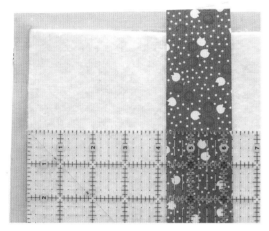

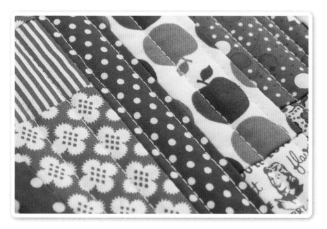

6 Zigzag stitch around the raw edge of the apple center and then appliqué two seeds on top (see Techniques: Appliqué).

3 Fold the twill tape in half, center the raw edges to the back top of the apple, and baste (tack).

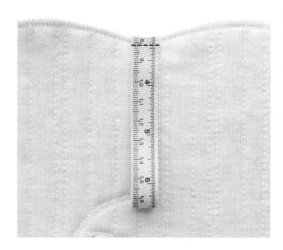

4 Use the 2in (5cm) wide bias-cut strip to make double-fold bias tape (see Techniques: Making Binding). Bind the potholder (see Techniques: Binding Curves). Finish the binding by hand or machine. Fold the twill tape up over the binding. Whip stitch in place by hand to the top layer of the binding to finish.

Keep It Simple

If using an air-drying fabric ink pen, you can make your quilt lines reappear or appear darker by placing a hot iron on them. The lines will fully fade within a couple of days.

To Finish

1 Place the apple template along the center line, matching up the apple center with that on the pattern, and trace the curved edge with a disappearing ink fabric pen. Flip over the template along the center line, finish tracing, and then cut out the apple with fabric shears.

2 Sew around the edge of the potholder with a machine zigzag stitch to help keep the edges neat and flat for the binding.

Cozy Four-Square
PILLOW

A playful, scrappy throw pillow is just the thing to add a pop of color to a chair or neutral décor. The front is made with a simple strip patchwork design and an easy quilt-as-you-go technique, while the back is finished with a linen envelope closure and cotton print binding. The sham is generously sized so that when the batting (wadding) shrinks with washing (giving it a gorgeous texture!) it will still fit well over the insert.

FINISHED DIMENSIONS:
17in (43cm) square, to fit a 16in (40.5cm) square pillow form. All seam allowances are ¼in (5mm) unless otherwise stated.

From Your
Scrap Bag

Basic tools
(see Equipment & Materials)

Assorted cotton prints in four colors for patchwork
Each print should be 9½in high (24cm) x 1¼in–3in wide (3cm–7.5cm)

Linen/cotton blend or solid cotton
One 17¾in x 19in (45cm x 48cm) piece

One 17¾in x 26in (45cm x 66cm) piece

Cotton print
Two strips 2in x 18in (5cm x 46cm) for double-fold binding

Cotton batting (wadding)
Four pieces each 10in (25.5cm) square

Cotton muslin
Four pieces each 10½in (26.5cm) square

Threads
All-purpose for piecing, assembling, and quilting, and hand quilting thread for binding and whip stitching

Pillow form
16in (40.5cm) square

To Make the Patchwork Front

1 Sew together several 9½in (24cm) cotton prints of various widths with the same main color, long sides together, to make a 9½in (24cm) square as shown. Press the seam allowances to one side. I recommend that the outside strips are a bit wide – 2½in (6.5cm) works well because they will be trimmed down and sewn later. Backstitch three or four stitches at the beginning and end of each seam to prevent the stitches from unraveling after trimming.

2 Make a quilt sandwich with a patchwork square, batting (wadding) square, and muslin square (see Techniques: Quilt Sandwich). Pin, then quilt the square in the same direction as the patchwork seams, with the quilting spaced about ⅜in (1cm) apart.

Chic Scrap Style

To make sure your pillow 'pops', include one or two strips of bold, medium- to large-scale prints to each square, either on a white or light background, or on a background a shade or two darker than the other strips.

3 Trim off the excess material and batting (wadding) to square the quilted block to 9¼in (23.5cm) square.

4 Repeat steps 1–3 for the three remaining batting (wadding) and muslin squares, using different colored prints for each square.

5 Arrange your blocks as desired, so that each block is at a 90-degree angle to the blocks next to it. Zigzag stitch the two inside edges of each block.

6 Sew the two squares on the left together with a ⅜in (1cm) seam allowance. Sew the other two squares together in the same way. Press the seam allowances open.

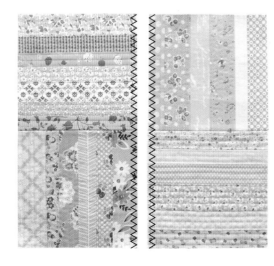

7 Place the two patchwork rectangles right sides together, making sure to carefully match the center seams, and sew together with a ⅜in (1cm) seam that is reinforced with backstitches in the center where all the seam allowances meet. Press the seam allowances open. Whip stitch the seam allowances to the muslin so they will lie flat after washing.

8 Square up and trim the pillow front to 17¾in (45cm) square.

To Make the Envelope Back and Finish

1 Fold and press the two rectangles of linen in half, so the large rectangle measures 17¾in x 13in (45cm x 33cm) and the small measures 17¾in x 9½in (45cm x 24cm). Use the 2in (5cm) wide bias-cut strip to make double-fold bias tape (see Techniques: Making Binding). Bind the folded edges of the linen pieces (see Techniques: Binding with Mitered Corners). Trim the tape to size.

2 Place the pillow front right side up, and then place the small linen rectangle on top of the pillow front, raw edges matching and with the binding toward the center.

3 Place the large linen rectangle on top of the first, raw edges matching the pillow front and binding parallel to that underneath. Sew all the way around the pillow with a ⅜in (1cm) seam.

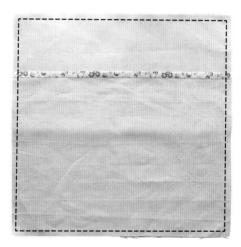

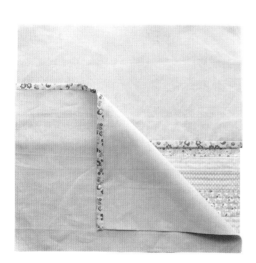

4 Trim the corners and then zigzag stitch the raw edges. Turn the sham right side out, press, and place the pillow form inside to finish.

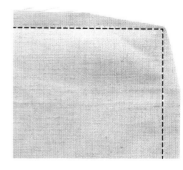

Keep It Simple
Use a larger gauge hand sewing needle and hand quilting thread to make it easier to sew through all the layers of fabric on the back of the pillow.

Scrappy Zigzag
QUILT

A traditional Roman Stripes block can look both classic and modern at the same time. With simple foundation piecing (you can do it!), you make two blocks at once, so this quilt comes together quickly. I used a combination of jelly roll pre-cuts and larger scraps of 1930s reproduction prints, paired with a mint green solid for the look of a feedsack quilt. Make the patchwork blocks with monochromatic prints like mine or super scrappy by mixing up a bunch of colors!

FINISHED DIMENSIONS:
52½in (133.5cm) square. All seam allowances are ¼in (5mm) unless otherwise stated.

From Your
Scrap Bag

Basic tools
(see Equipment & Materials)

Assorted cotton prints
Assorted color strips (pink, yellow, lavender, mint, blue, black, red) in various sizes, 1in–2½in wide x 11½in long (2.5cm–6.5cm x 29cm)

Prints pieced into single-fold tape for binding, 2½in x 3¼yd (6.5cm x 3m) in total

Cream or white cotton muslin
1¾yd (1.6m) of 44in (112cm) wide

Mint solid quilting cotton
1¾yd (1.6m) of 44in (112cm) wide

Cotton batting (wadding)
Twin-sized batting 72in x 90in (185cm x 230cm) (will leave enough left over for some small projects)

Backing fabric
About 56in (142cm) square – I pieced fat quarters and large remnants together

Threads
All-purpose thread in neutral color for piecing and matching color for quilting, and neutral hand quilting thread for sewing binding

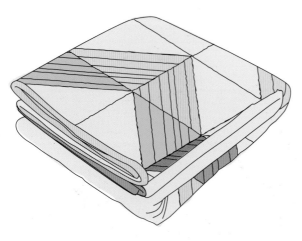

To Make the Quilt Blocks

1 From the cream or white cotton muslin cut thirty-two 7⅞in (20cm) squares. These will act as a foundation for your strip piecing. From the mint solid cotton cut thirty-two 7⅞in (20cm) squares.

2 Cut one strip of a cotton print 11½in (29.2cm) long. The width can vary, but it should be a minimum of 2½in (6.5cm) wide as it will lose approximately 1in (2.5cm) in width once sewn.

3 Place the cotton strip right side down, and mark the center of each short side with a disappearing ink fabric pen, as shown. Place a muslin square diagonally on top of it, so that two opposite corners line up with the marked centers of the cotton strip. Turn over the muslin and cotton pieces together.

4 Place another cotton print strip on top of the first, right sides together, lining up long sides of the strips, and pin. Make sure the center lines on the bottom strip still match the corners. The new cotton strip should be a little longer than the diagonal width of the muslin square, and at least 1in (2.5cm) wide. Sew the long edges of the strips together on top of the muslin. Backstitch each seam about ½in (1.3cm) onto the edges of the muslin so the stitching will not come apart once the blocks are trimmed to size.

5 Press the new cotton strip open. Continue sewing and pressing strips of random widths until one side of the muslin square is completely covered. Now rotate the square and sew the other half with strips.

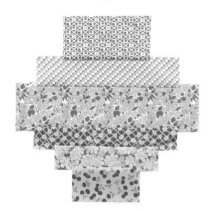

6 Turn over the patchwork square and trim to the size of the muslin square.

7 With a quilter's ruler and disappearing ink fabric pen, draw a diagonal line from corner to corner on the patchwork square, in the same direction as the stitched lines. Pin the patchwork square and a solid colored mint square right sides together. Sew a seam ¼in (5mm) to the right and left of the drawn line.

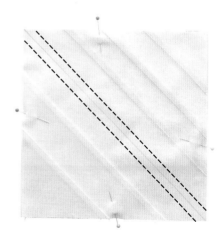

8 Using a quilter's ruler and rotary cutter, cut along the drawn line. Open up the two squares and press the seam allowances open. You've completed two blocks!

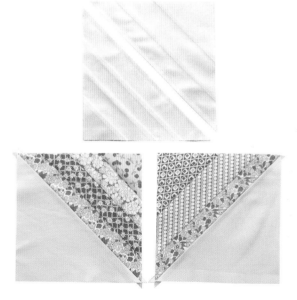

Keep It Simple
Pre-cut strips 2½in (6.5cm) wide (called jelly rolls by Moda) are the perfect width for making the scrappy binding on this quilt.

9 Repeat steps 2–8 for the remaining thirty-one solid and muslin blocks. Each pairing will yield two quilt blocks: I made six pink, six yellow, six lavender, five mint, four blue, three black, and two red.

10 You should now have sixty-four quilt blocks. Press and trim each block to 7in (18cm) square, making sure that the center line, where solid fabric meets printed fabric, lines up with the corners.

To Assemble the Quilt Front

1 Lay out the sixty-four blocks into four long zigzags (see diagram). Each row and each column should be eight blocks wide.

2 Sew the blocks into rows with a scant ¼in (5mm) seam allowance, starting at the top and sewing right side to left side. Press the seam allowances open.

3 Sew the rows together, again with a scant ¼in (5mm) seam, starting at the top and making sure the vertical seams line up. Press the seam allowances open.

4 Square up the quilt with a rotary cutter and straight edge/quilter's square.

To Finish

1 Make a backing for the quilt that is at least 2in (5cm) larger all around than the quilt front (about 56in/142cm square). I pieced fat quarters and large remnants together for my back.

2 Cut cotton batting (wadding) to 54in (137cm) square, make a quilt sandwich (see Techniques: Quilt Sandwich), pin with quilter's safety pins, and machine quilt. I marked evenly spaced lines with a disappearing ink fabric pen following the zigzag pattern of the blocks, and then sewed on top of the lines. Trim and square up the quilt.

3 Use the pieced binding strip to make double-fold bias tape (see Techniques: Making Binding). I used leftover jelly roll strips and triple stitched the ends together with 90-degree seams instead of diagonal seams. Press the seam allowances open.

4 Attach the binding using a ⅜in (1cm) seam allowance (see Techniques: Binding With Mitered Corners).

Sew Perfect

This cheerful quilt is made even more striking by the placement of contrasting tones and colors – go for maximum impact by placing lights against darks and complementary colors together.

SIMPLY SORTED

Simply Strippy
SEWING KIT

A cute clamshell-shape sewing kit is handy for quick fixes while traveling, or to keep in your bag for small projects away from home. Two pockets store all the necessities: needles, pins, thread, safety pins, fasteners, needle threader, folding scissors, and small measuring tape. The outside of the kit is made with little strips of cotton prints, while the inside has adorned linen pockets. Be creative with patchwork, fabric swatches, felts, and trims to personalize your kit any way you like!

FINISHED DIMENSIONS:
4½in high x 7½in wide (11.5cm x 19cm) when open. All seam allowances are ¼in (5mm) unless otherwise stated.

From Your
Scrap Bag

(Cut fabric pieces using the relevant Templates)

Basic tools
(see Equipment & Materials)

Assorted cotton prints
Strips for patchwork, cut as directed

5½in x 8½in (14cm x 21.5cm) piece for the backing

1½in x 22in (4cm x 56cm) of double-fold bias tape

Small scraps for decoration

Linen/cotton blend
Two 5in x 8in (12.5cm x 20.5cm) rectangles for pockets

Cotton batting (wadding)
About 6in x 9in (15cm x 23cm) for patchwork

Two 4in x 5in (10cm x 12.5cm) rectangles for pockets

Scraps of wool-blend felt

Fusible web

Sew-on snap fastener size 4

Threads
All-purpose thread for piecing and quilting, and hand quilting thread for sewing binding

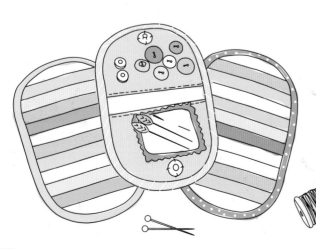

To Make the Patchwork Outer

1 Cut ten strips from various quilting cotton prints, each 1in x 5in (2.5cm x 12.5cm). Cut two strips from quilting cotton prints, each 1¾in x 5in (4.5cm x 12.5cm).

2 Arrange the twelve strips long sides together, with the wider 1¾in (4.5cm) strips on the ends. Sew the long sides together with a scant ¼in (5mm) seam and press each seam allowance to one side.

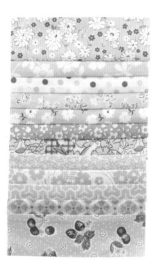

3 Cut a piece of batting (wadding) slightly larger than the patchwork. Make a quilt sandwich with the backing, batting, and patchwork rectangle (see Techniques: Quilt Sandwich), and quilt a scant ⅛in (3mm) from each seam.

4 Fold the quilted patchwork in half across the width, and place the sewing kit main pattern on top, arrows toward the fold. Double check to make sure you are using the correct template as the kit and pocket templates are very similar! Trace around the curve of the template. Cut out to make an elongated oval.

To Make the Pockets

1 Cut two 4in x 5in (10cm x 12.5cm) rectangles of batting (wadding). Place one batting rectangle on the wrong side of a linen rectangle. Fold over the linen, press, and topstitch ⅛in (3mm) from the folded edge. Repeat for the remaining batting and linen pieces.

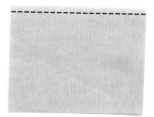

Chic Scrap Style

This little case is also great for carrying small electronic gear, such as an MP3 player, earbuds, and USB charger, or emergency on-the-go supplies – hair ties, cards, cash, and lip gloss all fit neatly inside!

2 Cut one pocket from each piece of linen, lining up the straight edge of the pocket template with the folded edge of the linen, as shown.

3 Now get creative with decorating your pockets! Cut a square of felt with scalloped fabric shears (or pinking shears) to store pins and needles, add a swatch of fabric backed with fusible web (to reduce frayed edges), and embellish with ribbons or other trims. Remember to leave at least ½in (1.3cm) space on the straight sides and 1in (2.5cm) on the curved ends to accommodate the binding and snaps.

To Finish

1 Place the quilted patchwork backing side up, and then place the pockets on each end, right sides facing up. Pin, and then zigzag stitch around the edges.

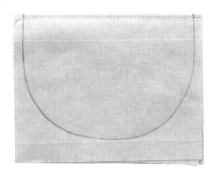

2 Prepare the double-fold tape for binding (see Techniques: Preparing Bias-Cut Strips for Binding). Bind the sewing kit with the double-fold bias tape (see Techniques: Binding Curves).

3 Separate the sew-on snap fastener, and sew one side securely to each of the linen pockets, centered on the curve, just above the binding.

4 Sew on buttons and fill your kit with sewing goodies!

Sew Perfect
Mark snap and button placements first with a fabric pen, as this makes aiming your needle through the pockets much easier!

On-a-Roll Crochet
HOOK HOLDER

Make a pretty, quilted crochet hook case to match your sewing kit. Constructed similarly to the Strippy Sewing Kit, this is another great scrap-busting project for narrow, leftover strips of fabric. The outside of the roll is made with coordinating quilting cotton prints, while a linen pocket and flap on the inside stores crochet hooks and accessories. Tuck your hooks under the flap, then roll up and tie to keep your crochet supplies safe and tidy.

FINISHED DIMENSIONS:
7½in high x 10in wide (19cm x 25.5cm). All seam allowances are ¼in (5mm) unless otherwise stated.

From Your
Scrap Bag

(Cut fabric pieces using the relevant Templates)

Basic tools
(see Equipment & Materials)

Assorted cotton prints
Strips for patchwork, cut as directed

8½in x 10½in (21.5cm x 27cm) for pocket backing

1¾in x 30in (4.5cm x 76cm) double-fold bias tape for binding

1½in x 30in (4cm x 76cm) double-fold tape for ties, not bias-cut

Linen/cotton blend fabric
One piece for pocket

One piece for flap

Lightweight fusible interfacing
8in x 10in (20.5cm x 25.5cm) for pocket

Lightweight sew-in stabilizer
¼yd (0.25m) for pocket and flap

All-purpose thread
For piecing and quilting

Cotton batting (wadding)
11½in x 9½in (29cm x 24cm) approximately

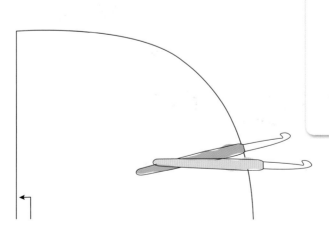

To Make the Patchwork Outer

1 Cut ten strips from various quilting cotton prints, each 1¼in x 8½in (3.2cm x 21.5cm). Cut two strips from quilting cotton prints, each 1¾in x 8½in (4.5cm x 21.5cm).

2 Arrange the twelve strips, long sides together, with the wider 1¾in (4.5cm) strips on the ends. Sew the long sides together with a scant ¼in (5mm) seam and press each seam allowance to one side.

3 Place the patchwork on top of the piece of batting (wadding), which is cut slightly larger, pin together, and quilt a scant ⅛in (3mm) from each seam.

4 Fold the quilted patchwork in half across the width, and then place the main piece template on top, arrows toward the folded fabric. Trace around the curve of the template and cut to make an elongated oval.

To Make the Pocket and Flap

1 Cut one pocket piece and one flap from linen/cotton blend by folding over the fabric and placing the template arrows toward the fold. Trace and cut only around the curved sides. Cut another pocket piece from quilting cotton for the pocket backing. Attach same-sized fusible interfacing to the wrong side of the cotton pocket.

2 Fold the linen pocket piece in half lengthwise, wrong sides together, and press – this will be the pocket. Using the folded pocket as a template, cut a piece of lightweight stabilizer and place it inside the folded linen.

3 Fold the linen flap in half lengthwise, wrong sides together, and press. Using the folded flap as a template, cut a piece of stabilizer the same size and place it inside the flap.

4 Place the raw edges of the flap and pocket on the top and bottom of the pocket backing and pin on the right side. Use a quilting ruler to make sure the folded edges of the flap and pocket are parallel. Baste (tack) the pieces in place along the raw edges.

5 Mark lines for the pocket seams with a quilter's ruler and disappearing fabric marker, as shown.

- Mark the first line 2¼in (5.5cm) from the left side.
- Mark the next four lines ½in (1.3cm) apart.
- Mark the next two lines ⅝in (1.5cm) apart.
- Mark the next three lines ¾in (2cm) apart. The last line should be about 2¼in (5.5cm) from the right side.

Now triple stitch each line, from the bottom raw edge to the top folded edge.

To Assemble and Finish

1 Place the wrong side of the assembled pocket piece onto the batting (wadding) side of the quilted patchwork. Pin, then zigzag stitch all the way around the raw edges.

2 To make the ties, hand stitch closed two pieces of 1½in (4cm) double-fold tape using hand quilting thread and ladder stitches, each with one end pressed under ½in (1.3cm). One tie should be cut 11½in (29cm), the other 17in (43cm). Stack the two ties with the shorter tie on top, centered on one of the short curved sides of the patchwork, and baste (tack) in place.

3 Prepare the 1¾in (4.5cm) wide double-fold tape for binding (see Techniques: Preparing Bias-Cut Strips for Binding). Bind the crochet hook roll with the bias tape (see Techniques: Binding Curves). Make sure the ties stay straight and out of the way during the machine sewing.

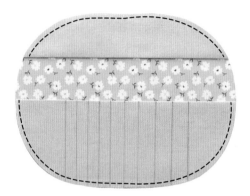

Scrap Patch
PINCUSHION

This cute pincushion is a great project to showcase your favorite fabric scraps, and would make a pretty gift for a friend who is just beginning to sew. Whether using a monochromatic color scheme or a full palette of colors, it is sure to brighten up any sewing space! A little bag of crushed walnuts or fine sand inside the pincushion helps to keep pins super sharp and protect your beautiful fabrics from snags while pinning.

FINISHED DIMENSIONS:
2in high x 4½ wide (5cm x 11.5cm). All seam allowances are 5mm (¼in) unless otherwise stated.

From Your
Scrap Bag

(Cut fabric pieces using the relevant Templates *)

Basic tools
(see Equipment & Materials)

Assorted cotton prints
Ten pincushion wedges, each from a different print *

One circle for fabric button

Linen/cotton blend
One pincushion bottom *

One 1¾in x 34in (4.5cm x 86cm) rectangle for pleated edge

All-purpose thread
in a neutral color

¾in (2cm) fabric covered button kit

Embroidery floss (cotton)
for sewing the button on

Darning needle

Stuffing material (polyfill)

Cotton muslin or solid fabric
Two circles for walnut/ sand bag (optional) *

Crushed walnuts or fine sand
(optional)

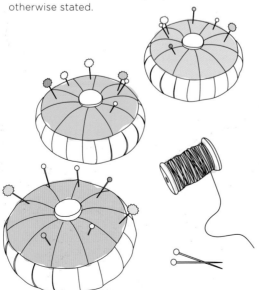

To Assemble the Patchwork Top

1 Lay out your ten wedges in a circle. Starting at any point, sew five wedges into a half circle – working clockwise, place two wedges right sides together, right piece on top of left piece, and sew down the right side. Open the fabric and press each seam allowance to the right.

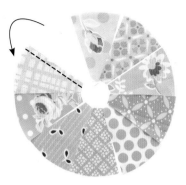

To Pleat the Edge

1 On the long edge of the linen rectangle, make ¼in (5mm) pleats about ½in (1.3cm) apart, starting 2in (5cm) from a short side. To make pleats, pinch about ½in (1.3cm) of fabric with your fingers and fold it to the left, as shown. The pleats should not overlap. Pin each pleat at the top and bottom, and press them in place. You may not need the entire length of the linen strip, just about 13in (33cm) of pleating plus the 2in (5cm) extra before pleating.

2 Starting again, but continuing around the circle, sew the remaining five wedges together into a separate half circle.

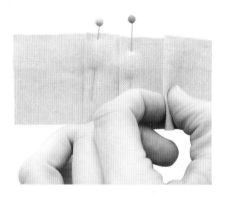

3 Place the circle halves right sides together, pin, and sew along the straight side. Open up the circle and press the seam allowance open the best you can – it will be a little bulky in the middle.

2 Machine baste (tack) the pleats into position along the top and bottom of the strip, ⅛in (3mm) from the edge, keeping the edges as straight as possible.

3 Square up the pleated rectangle, then cut it to 12¾in (32.5cm) in length. Trim off some of the first 2in (5cm) and rip out a pleat seam if necessary so you have a single layer of fabric to sew through ¼in (5mm) from each end. Sew the short ends, right sides together, to make a loop and press the seam allowance open.

4 Carefully pin the right side of the pleated loop to the right side of the patchwork circle. Adjust the pins until the fabrics match. Sew together with a ¼in (5mm) seam, all the way around the circle.

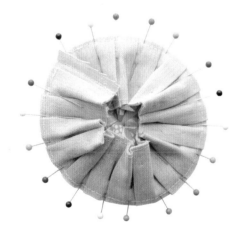

5 Pin the right side of the pleated loop to the right side of the pincushion bottom as you did with the top, and sew together, leaving a 2in (5cm) hole for turning through.

6 Press and trim the seam allowances, top and bottom, except around the turning hole, then turn the pincushion right side out.

To Finish

1 Place the muslin circles together and triple stitch around the edge, leaving a 1in (2.5cm) hole unsewn. Fill with crushed walnuts or fine sand, leaving enough space to fit your sewing machine foot. Tape or otherwise seal the open side and then finish sewing the circle closed.

2 Insert the crushed walnut bag into the top of the pincushion, and then stuff the rest of the pincushion with polyfill. Turn the pincushion over and add a thin layer of polyfill on top of the walnuts. Close the hole with ladder stitches.

3 Make a fabric-covered button according to the package instructions. Use fusible interfacing on the back of the button fabric if the fabric is a light color so the metal button does not show through.

4 Mark the center of the bottom of the pincushion. Sew the fabric-covered button to the top of the pincushion with embroidery floss and a darning needle, sewing all the way through to the bottom and back through to the top several times, pulling the thread taut so the button sinks into the pincushion a bit. Tie securely and trim the floss to finish.

Craft on the Go
TOTE BAG

A pretty tote makes every outing more fun and this one is great for taking projects out and about with you. The patchwork is comprised of many thin strips of fabric, making this a great scrap-busting project. Cotton/linen blend paired with pastel prints is lovely for a spring or summer bag, or use corduroy and darker jewel-toned prints for a fall or winter tote.

FINISHED DIMENSIONS:
12¾in high x 15in wide x 4in deep (32.5cm x 38cm x 10cm). All seam allowances are ¼in (5mm) unless otherwise stated.

From Your
Scrap Bag

Basic tools
(see Equipment & Materials)

Assorted cotton prints
Plenty of strips for patchwork, each 1½in (4cm) wide and random lengths – I used about forty strips for each side of the tote, between 3in–7in (7.5cm–18cm) long

Two pieces of the same cotton print, each 15in x 16in (38cm x 40.5cm) for the tote lining

One print 10½in x 16½in (27 x 42cm) for the pocket

One print 1½in x 17in (4cm x 43cm) pressed into double-fold tape for pocket binding

Linen/cotton blend
Two pieces, each 4½in x 16in (11.5cm x 40.5cm) for tote base

Two pieces, each 4in x 41in (10cm x 104cm) for straps

One bias-cut strip 2in x 36in (5cm x 91.5cm) for tote binding

Cotton batting (wadding)
Two pieces, each 17in (43cm) x about 21in (53.5cm), depending on length of patchwork strips

Lightweight fusible interfacing
Two pieces, each 4in x 42in (10cm x 107cm) for backing straps

All-purpose thread

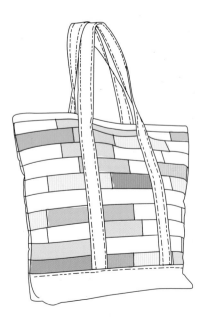

To Make and Quilt the Patchwork

1 Sew 1½in (4cm) wide cotton print strips into approximately 18in–20in (45.5cm–51cm) lengths and lay out the strips into ten rows, so that you will be able to cut the patchwork to 16in (40.5cm) wide after assembly. Position the rows so that seams are staggered as shown. Pin and sew the rows together with a scant ¼in (5mm) seam allowance.

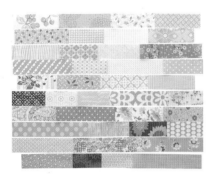

2 Place the patchwork on a piece of batting (wadding), with the top edge of the patchwork 1in (2.5cm) below the top of the batting, which should then extend about 5in (12.5cm) below the patchwork. Machine quilt ⅛in (3mm) above and below each long seam.

3 Repeat steps 1–3 to make the other side of the bag.

4 Square up and cut each of quilted patchwork pieces to 16in (40.5cm) wide. Do *not* trim the top and bottom of the batting (wadding).

To Make the Straps

1 Adhere fusible interfacing to the wrong side of the strap pieces. Press the strap pieces in the same way as making double-fold tape (see Techniques: Making Binding), leaving a space of ¼in (5mm) between the long raw edges when folded.

2 Re-fold one of the straps and mark a point 9½in (24cm) from each end with a disappearing ink fabric pen. Topstitch the strap ⅛in (3mm) from each side, between the two marks. Repeat for the other strap.

3 Place a strap on one of the patchwork pieces, raw edge of the strap aligned with the bottom raw edge of the patchwork, 5in (12.5cm) from the left edge of the patchwork. Bend the strap around (being careful not to twist it), and place the other raw edge of the strap along the bottom edge of the patchwork, 5in (12.5cm) from the other side. Pin in place. Repeat for the other strap and patchwork piece.

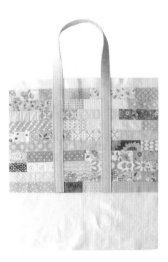

4 Triple stitch the straps to the patchwork, ⅛in (3mm) from the edges of the strap. Start at the raw edge and sew upward, turn at the top of the patchwork strip second from the top, sew across the strap, turn ⅛in (3mm) from the side and sew back down to the bottom of the strap. Then sew the opposite end of the strap. Repeat for the other strap.

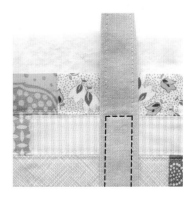

5 Place a 4½in x 16in (11.5cm x 40.5cm) linen piece along the bottom edge of the patchwork, right sides together and matching the raw edges. Pin and sew together along the bottom edge. Press the linen down and triple stitch ⅛in (3mm) from the top edge of the linen. Repeat for the other piece of linen and patchwork.

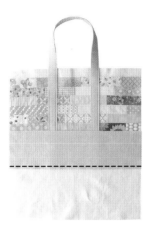

6 Square up and trim the batting (wadding) from above the patchwork and below the linen on both pieces, being careful to avoid cutting the straps.

To Make the Lining and Pocket

1 Fold the pocket fabric in half lengthwise, so it measures 5¼in x 16½in (13.5cm x 42cm). Bind the long raw edges of the pocket together with 1½in (4cm) wide cotton print binding tape. Trim the binding to fit the pocket width.

2 Place the pocket on the right side of a lining piece across the 16in (40.5cm) width, with the binding edge 5in (12.5cm) from the top, and pin. The edges should extend ¼in (5mm) beyond each side of the lining. Triple stitch the pocket to the lining along the folded bottom edge of the pocket, and then trim the pocket sides to match the width of the lining. Baste (tack) the left and right sides of the pocket to the edges of the lining.

3 Mark stitch lines for pocket dividers for phone, pen and so on with a disappearing ink fabric pen and triple stitch *slowly* from the top to the bottom of the pocket.

To Assemble

1 Place the patchwork tote pieces right sides together, matching the seams on the edges, and pin. Mark and cut a 2in (5cm) square from the left and right lower corners of the pieces (on the linen end). Triple stitch the patchwork pieces along the left and right sides and bottom. Leave the top edge and the inside edges of the cut-outs unsewn.

2 Pull open one of the 2in (5cm) cut-outs. Match up the seams in the center, and flatten the seam allowances in opposite directions. Pin and triple stitch across the raw edge with a ¼in (5mm) seam allowance. Repeat for the other cut-out, making sure the seam allowances are folded in the same direction along the bottom of the tote. Press the seam allowances open about 1in (2.5cm) on the top sides of the tote.

3 Repeat steps 1–3 above to assemble the lining pieces.

4 Turn the patchwork tote right side out and place the lining inside the tote, wrong sides together, and matching side seams. Pin and machine baste (tack) the lining to the outer tote ⅛in (3mm) from the top edge.

5 Bind the tote with the bias-cut linen strip (see Techniques: Binding Curves). Finish the binding by hand or machine.

CHILD'S PLAY

Pajama Bear
SOFTIES

With a cute expression and cozy pajamas, these little bears make bedtime fun! You'll love all the details – the pleated ears, the pajama flap, the sweet felt collar, and buttons. One of my favorite materials for making soft critters is fur-colored corduroy as it has a great texture and contrasts nicely with bright cotton prints. Pair with a favorite bedtime storybook for a cute baby shower gift. You can easily enlarge or reduce the patterns to make a whole family of bears.

FINISHED DIMENSIONS:
11in (28cm) high. All seam allowances are ¼in (5mm) unless otherwise stated.

From Your
Scrap Bag

(Cut fabric pieces using the relevant Templates *)

Basic tools
(see Equipment & Materials)

Corduroy fabric
Two heads, four ears, and four paws *

Cotton prints
Two pajamas from main print *

Four sleeves from main print, two cut with pattern right side up, two right side down *

Two pajama flaps from coordinating print *

Wool blend felt in assorted colors
Two eye whites, two pupils, one muzzle, one nose, two cheeks, one or two collar pieces *

Lightweight fusible interfacing
Two heads and two pajamas *

Four small buttons (optional)
Use buttons cut from felt if making for a young child

Embroidery floss (cotton)
For sewing buttons

All-purpose thread
Neutral for inside of bear, and colors to match eye whites, pupils, muzzle, nose, cheeks, collar, and pajama flap

Stuffing material

To Assemble the Bear

1 Place the two pajama flap pieces right sides together and sew around the edges, leaving a 1in (2.5cm) hole on one side for turning. Trim the corners, turn right side out, and press.

3 Match the short straight sides of the four paws and four arms where marked with dots on the templates, right sides together, and sew across the short straight sides as shown. Press the seam allowances toward the paws. Pair up matching sleeve pieces, then triple stitch around the long and curved sides, leaving a 1in (2.5cm) hole unsewn on the longest side. Do *not* sew the angled short edge of the arm. Trim seam allowances, turn right side out, and press.

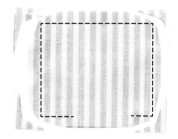

Sew Perfect

When cutting two pieces of fabric from one template, fold the fabric onto itself, trace around the template, and then cut both pieces at the same time. Line up the arrow on the sleeve template with the print on the pajama fabric before cutting, so the print goes in the same direction on all pieces.

4 Fuse the bumpy side of the fusible interfacing to the wrong sides of the head and pajama pieces. Do *not* place the iron directly on the interfacing or the front of the corduroy.

5 Edge stitch the felt facial features onto the bear's face. Sew the muzzle, eye whites, and cheeks first, then the nose and pupils on top, all with matching thread.

2 Place two ear pieces right sides together and triple stitch around the curved edge. Trim the seam allowances and turn right side out. Repeat for the other set of ears. Pleat the center of each ear in opposite directions with ¼in (5mm) pleats, and then baste (tack) the pleats in place.

6 Center and edge stitch the collar piece(s) on the top of one of the pajama pieces – this is the pajama front. The top of the triangle collar pieces (for the boy bear) should overlap ¼in (5mm) in the center. On the right side of the other pajama piece, place the flap according to the pattern markings and topstitch in place – this is the pajama back.

8 Sew two buttons to the front of the bear and two to the pajama flap with three strands of embroidery floss.

9 Place the ears and arms on the bear where indicated on the pattern, facing inward, and pointing toward the feet. The arms should extend ½in (1.3cm) off the sides of the bear. Baste (tack) in place.

Keep it Simple
Scalloped fabric shears makes cutting the girl bear's collar a breeze!

10 Place the bear front and back right sides together, pin, and triple stitch all the way around, leaving a 2in (5cm) hole under one arm for turning. Trim the seam allowances, cutting notches into the curve between the legs.

7 Place the straight edges of the head front and pajama front right sides together, pin, and triple stitch across the straight edge. Do the same for the head back and pajama back. Open up the fabrics and press the seam allowances toward the head.

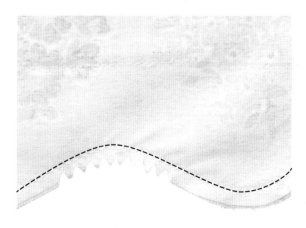

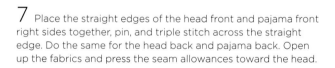

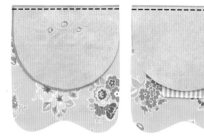

11 Turn the bear right side out and stuff the body and arms. Close all the holes by hand with a ladder stitch to finish.

Owl See You Around
BOOKENDS

Hoot hoot! These super easy owls stitch up quickly and the simple shape makes for a perfect introduction to softie making. With just lightweight stuffing inside, these wise little birds are adorable toys, but with lots of weighted filling, they are not only cute but helpful, too, perched on a bookshelf as a bookend, or greeting visitors as a doorstop.

FINISHED DIMENSIONS:
7½in (19cm) high. All seam allowances are ¼in (5mm) unless otherwise stated.

From Your
Scrap Bag

(Cut fabric pieces using the relevant Templates *)

Basic tools
(see Equipment & Materials)

Cotton prints
Two wings, right and left *

One body ¼yd (0.25m) for owl back *

Medium wale corduroy
One body ¼yd (0.25m) for owl front *

Wool blend felt various colors
Two feet and one beak, two eye whites, two irises, two pupils *

Fusible web
Small pieces for backing wings

Lightweight fusible interfacing
Two owl bodies ¼yd (0.25m) *

Threads
All-purpose thread to match beak and feet, eye felts, appliqué on wings, and neutral for inside the owl, and hand quilting thread for closing the stuffing hole

Stuffing material

Nylon tights or trouser socks

Weighted material
Dried beans or rice

Ultra-firm interfacing (Peltex)
Two rectangles 2¾in x 3⅞in (7cm x 10cm) for owl base

To Make the Front and Base

1 Fuse fusible interfacing to the wrong side of the corduroy owl body. Repeat for the other interfacing and cotton owl bodies.

2 Back the two wings, right and left, with fusible web. Place the wings onto the corduroy owl front according to the pattern placement and fuse in place with a hot iron (see Techniques: Appliqué). Zigzag stitch around the curved edges of the wings.

3 Place the eye whites on the owl according to the pattern, and edge stitch with matching thread. Sew the irises next, and then the pupils on top.

4 Edge stitch the feet and beak onto the owl front with matching thread according to the pattern.

5 Place the two ultra-firm interfacing rectangles together and edge stitch together to make a base for the owl.

2 Pull apart one of the cut-outs, match the center seams and finger press the seam allowances in opposite directions. Triple stitch across this straight edge. Repeat for the other side, making sure that the bottom seam allowance lies flat.

To Assemble

1 Place the owl front and back right sides together and pin. Triple stitch around the owl *except* for the square cut-outs in each bottom corner, and leave a 3in (7.5cm) hole for stuffing in the middle of one side.

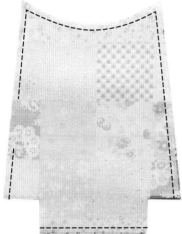

3 Trim the corners of the ears, taking care not to snip into the seams, and cut notches into the inner curve of the head. Turn the owl right side out. Use a chopstick to push out the ears, but be careful not to stretch the fabric.

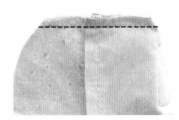

Keep it Simple
If making an owl doorstop, try bags filled with sand to add extra weight.

4 Place the firm interfacing base into the bottom of the owl, fitting it between the side seam allowances. Fill a nylon stocking with a few handfuls of dried beans or rice, securely tie the top, cut above the knot, and insert it into the base. Stuff the top of the head and ears with stuffing material, then fill in the body and spaces around the beans or rice with more stuffing. Close the hole by hand with a ladder stitch and hand quilting thread.

Oh Sew Cute
BABY BIBS

Your little one will be best dressed at the dinner table wearing this cute patchwork bib with pretty rick rack trim. An absorbent flannel inner layer helps keep baby dry, and bias tape ties add a vintage touch. Use outgrown infant clothes or flannel blankets to make a 'new' hand-me-down gift, or dig out a few of your favorite sewing scraps that you and baby can both savor over mealtime!

FINISHED DIMENSIONS:
10½in high x 9½in wide (26.7cm x 24.1cm) for 3 months+. All seam allowances are ¼in (5mm) unless otherwise stated.

From Your
Scrap Bag

(Cut fabric pieces using the relevant Templates)

Basic tools
(see Equipment & Materials)

Assorted cotton prints
Two rectangles each 2½in x 2in (6.5cm x 5cm) for patchwork

Four 2in (5cm) squares for patchwork

Two rectangles of the same print 10⅝in x 7½in (27cm x 19cm) and 10⅝in x 3in (27cm x 7.5cm) for bib front

One rectangle 10¾in x 11¾in (27.5cm x 30cm) for bib back

1½in x 2yd (4cm x 2m) bias-cut fabric strip for binding and ties

Cotton flannel
10¾in x 11¾in (27.5cm x 30cm) for inner layer of bib

Rick rack
½in (1.3cm) wide x 20in (51cm) approx, for decoration (optional)

Threads
All-purpose thread for piecing and quilting, hand quilting thread for sewing binding, and embroidery floss for running stitches (optional)

To Make the Patchwork

1 Place the six cotton prints into a row, lining up the 2in (5cm) edges, and with the longer rectangles on the ends. Sew the pieces into a row, and press the seam allowances open.

2 Place rick rack along the bottom 10⅝in (27cm) edge of the larger bib front rectangle, and the top 10⅝in (27cm) edge of the smaller bib front rectangle, and then baste (tack) in place very close to the edges.

4 Sew the bottom of the patchwork to the top of the smaller rectangle. Press each seam allowance toward the patchwork so the rick rack lies facing away from the pieced fabrics. If omitting the rick rack, press the seam allowances away from the patchwork.

3 Sew the top of the patchwork to the bottom of the larger rectangle, with the rick rack sandwiched between the layers.

Keep it Simple
A hand-sewn running stitch with embroidery floss above and below the patchwork is a cute alternative to rick rack trim.

To Quilt and Finish

1 Make a quilt sandwich with the backing, flannel inner layer, and pieced bib front (see Techniques: Quilt Sandwich).

2 Stitch in the ditch (in the seams) between the patchwork and rick rack to quilt the layers together. If omitting the rick rack, stitch in the ditch on top of the patchwork.

3 Center the bib template onto the patchwork, matching the parallel lines on the template to the patchwork row, and matching the center line of the template with the center vertical patchwork seam. Trace the curved edges of the pattern with a disappearing ink fabric pen, and then flip over the pattern to trace the other half of the bib. Cut out with fabric shears.

4 Zigzag stitch the edge of the bib over the rick rack and patchwork to keep the layers together and prevent the rick rack from fraying. Add running stitches above and below the patchwork if desired. Tie off securely on each side.

5 Press the bias-cut fabric strip into double-fold tape (see Techniques: Making Binding). Cut a 14in (35.5cm) length of the bias tape. Sew it to the inner curve of the bib front and finish by hand on the back (see Techniques: Binding Curves). Trim the binding to match the points at the top of the bib.

6 Find the center of the remaining bias tape, unfold it and hold in place along the outer raw edges of the bib front with binding clips, centered on the bottom of the bib. Trim the tape to 12½in (32cm) longer than the top points of the bib on each side. Press the short ends under ½in (1.3cm), then re-fold and press again.

7 Attach the bias tape to the outside of the bib and finish sewing by hand. Tuck in the little raw edges at the ends of the ties with a needle and stitch across the tops to enclose them.

Sweet Sailor
DRESS DOLL

Ahoy! Your little one will love going on adventures with this stylish little sailor, and you will love practicing your doll-making skills with loads of fun details. From the cute nautical-inspired outfit, to the sweet side ponytail, and the twinkle in her hand-embroidered eyes, you can practice several easy techniques that are useful for many sewing projects.

FINISHED DIMENSIONS:
18in (45.5cm) high. All seam allowances are ¼in (5mm) unless otherwise stated.

From Your
Scrap Bag

(Cut fabric pieces using relevant Templates *)

Basic tools
(see Equipment & Materials)

Assorted cotton prints
Two dresses from main navy/white print *

2in x 2½in (5cm x 6.5cm) rectangle from striped navy/white print for dickey

Four socks from yellow print *

Solid cotton for skin ⅓yd (0.3m)
One head *

Four arms, cut two sets with fabric folded *

Four legs, cut two sets with fabric folded *

Lightweight fusible interfacing ½yd (0.5m)
One head and two dresses

Fusible web
For backing the dickey rectangle

Wool blend felt in brown, white, black, and red

Four small buttons

Rick rack ½in x 15in (1.3cm x 38cm)

Threads
All-purpose threads to match fabrics, neutral for inside doll, and quilting thread for closing holes

Embroidery floss (cotton) in black and white

Stuffing material

To Make the Face and Hair

1 From brown felt cut one hair piece, one head and two ponytails. From white felt cut one bib. From black felt cut two shoe fronts and two shoe backs. From red felt cut one piece 2⅞in x ⅞in (7.5cm x 2.2cm) for bow and two 1⅜in x ⅝in (3.5cm x 1.5cm) for bow ends.

2 Attach fusible interfacing to the wrong side of the cotton head. Hand embroider the face on the right side, using all six strands of black embroidery floss. For the eyes, sew backstitches around the circle of the eye, then fill the circle with satin stitches. Sew backstitches for eyelashes, nose, and mouth. Use three strands of white floss to sew a single stitch in the upper right of each eye, for a shine.

3 Place the hair felt on the right side of the cotton head and edge stitch all the way around. Quilt the hair with stitched lines ½in (1.3cm) apart, following the curve of the hairline above the eyes and working upward as shown. Quilt short lines from the lowest quilt line to the side of the head. Remember to backstitch the beginning and end of each seam.

4 Quilt the head cut from felt (the back of the head) by sewing a shallow curved line across the middle of the felt. Using this line as a guide, quilt ½in (1.3cm) spaced lines to fill in the rest of the head above and below.

5 Place the two felt ponytails together so all edges line up, and edge stitch the curved edges. Make a ¼in (5mm) pleat on the straight edge, flatten it with your fingers, and machine baste (tack) in place.

Sew Perfect
When sewing the legs together, use thread to match the shoes for sewing around the shoes, and neutral for rest of the legs. Do the same for the hair and body when sewing the entire doll together.

To Make the Arms and Legs

1 Match the two sets of arms, right sides facing together, and triple stitch the long sides and curves. Leave the short straight edge unsewn, as well as a 1½in–2in (4cm–5cm) hole near each hand for stuffing. Trim the seam allowances with pinking shears. Turn the arms right side out, and then carefully fold under and press the fabric around the stuffing holes.

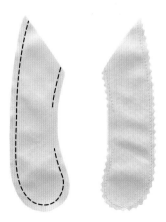

2 Place all the cotton print sock pieces right sides facing up. Next, place all of the cotton leg pieces on top of the socks, right sides together, bottom of leg to top of sock (marked with a dot on the pattern pieces). Triple stitch across each of these short straight edges, open the fabrics, and press the seam allowances toward the socks.

3 Place the four shoe pieces (two fronts, two backs) on the four sock pieces and pin. Edge stitch all the way around the shoes with matching thread, and remember to also edge stitch the inner cut-out on the shoe fronts.

To Make the Dress

1 Fuse the interfacing to the wrong side of the dress pieces, making sure the iron does not directly touch the interfacing.

2 Back the 2in x 2½in (5cm x 6.5cm) rectangle of striped navy/white print with fusible web. Center a long edge of this dickey rectangle on the top of one of the dress pieces, adhesive side of the dickey to right side of dress, and fuse in place. Zigzag stitch the dickey around the sides and bottom.

3 Center the felt bib over the dickey, aligning the short straight edges with the top of the dress, and edge stitch in place with matching thread.

4 Match the two sets of legs, shoe front to shoe back, and pin. Triple stitch around the edges, *except* leave the top short edge unsewn, as well as a hole 1½in–2in (4cm–5cm) on one side of each leg, above the socks (similar to sewing the arms). Trim seam allowances, turn right side out, and press.

6 Sew four buttons onto the dress front with embroidery floss, in centered pairs below the bib.

To Assemble

1 Pin the head front and dress front right sides together, aligning the straight edges and triple stitch across the straight edge. Press the seam allowance toward the head. Repeat for the back of the head and dress back, but press the seam allowance toward the dress.

4 Cut a triangle out of one side of both 1⅜in x ⅝in (3.5cm x 1.5cm) felt rectangles, and then zigzag the short straight edges in place with matching thread. The bow will be added after assembly. This is the dress front.

5 Place rick rack on the right sides of both dress pieces, with the top edge 1¾in (4.5cm) from the bottom of the dresses. Stitch in place along the center of the trim with matching thread.

2 Place the ponytail on the doll's head, just above the neck seam, so that the tip is pointing upward and the straight edges just hang off the edge of the head. Pin and machine baste (tack) in place.

3 Place the arms on the doll, with the top of the arms ⅛in (3mm) below the neck seam, hands pointing toward the rick rack, and curving outward. The edges of the arms should hang off the doll ½in (1.3cm). Pin and baste (tack).

Sew Perfect

Rick rack can be a little tricky to sew. To make sure your rick rack stays straight, trace a line with a disappearing ink fabric pen where the top edge should be, so you can line up the rick rack and make adjustments as it tries to shift while sewing.

4 Place the legs on the doll, shoe fronts facing the dress, toes pointing toward the face, and short ends hanging off the edge ½in (1.3cm). The legs should be centered and spaced ⅜in–½in (1cm–1.3cm) apart. Pin and baste (tack).

5 Place the back of the doll on top of the front, with right sides facing together. Pin, taking special care to match up the neck seams on each side and keeping the shoes clear of the seam allowance. Triple stitch all the way around, except for a 3in (7.5cm) hole under one of the arms for turning and stuffing.

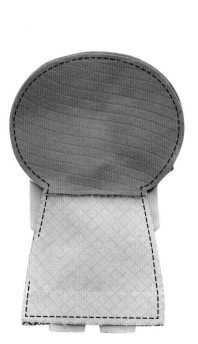

6 Trim the seam allowances with pinking shears, except around the turning hole. Carefully cut a notch in the seam allowance where the head meets the body, just under or above the neck seam. Do not cut into the stitching.

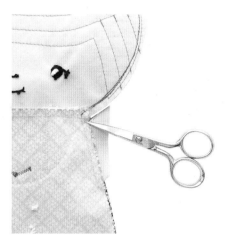

7 Turn the doll right side out and touch up wrinkles with an iron, being careful not to place the iron directly on the felt. Use a chopstick to gently push out all the seams.

To Finish

1 Pinch the red felt rectangle in the middle to look like a bow. Hand sew through the center several times, knot securely to hold it in place, and trim the thread.

2 Sew the bow to the front of the dress by hand, over the tops of the ties. Reach inside the doll while sewing to help guide the needle. Sew several stitches through the back of the bow and through the bib/dress. Knot securely and then trim the thread.

3 Stuff the body, arms, and legs, and then close all the holes by hand with ladder stitch and hand quilting thread.

Simple Cloud + Raindrop
HOOPS

This easy embroidery hoop art is a sure way to brighten up any room on a rainy day. Pairing simple appliqué with favorite fabric prints creates wall art that goes together as quick as lightning. Raw-edged appliqué gives the hoops the artsy feel of a sketch, and the hoops are finished on the back with a simple and pretty technique.

FINISHED DIMENSIONS:
Variable, according to hoop size. All seam allowances are ¼in (5mm) unless otherwise stated.

From Your
Scrap Bag

(Cut fabric pieces using the relevant Templates *)

Basic tools
(see Equipment & Materials)

Wood embroidery hoops
One 9in (23cm), one 6in (15cm), one 5in (12.5cm), one 4in (10cm), and two 3in (7.5cm)

Assorted cotton prints
Main prints and backing fabrics, cut as directed

One cloud and one of each raindrop from coordinating fabrics *

Fusible web
For backing the cloud and raindrop appliqués

Wool-blend felt for cheeks *

Cotton batting (wadding)
In sizes slightly bigger than the hoops

Threads
All-purpose thread in black, and to match the cheek felt, and hand quilting thread in a neutral color

Embroidery floss (cotton) in black

Medium-weight chipboard (mountboard)
To make circles the same size as the hoops

74

To Make the Hoop Front

The following instructions describe how to make the cloud hoop. The raindrop hoop instructions are the same except for omitting the face embroidery.

1 Cut the main fabric to a circle about 3in (7.5cm) larger all around than the 9in (23cm) hoop. Smaller hoops will not require such a large diameter of fabric, just enough so that the fabric can be secured on the back of the hoop under the backing without slipping out.

2 Use the template to cut a cloud from fabric and backed with fusible web (see Techniques: Appliqué). Remove the paper backing and trace the face onto the cloud with a disappearing ink fabric pen by holding up the template and fabric to a sunny window or light box.

3 Use the hoop to help determine the center of the large fabric circle, and then place the cloud a little below and to the right of center. Raindrops should be centered in their hoops. Fuse the cloud to the main fabric, with the adhesive side of the cloud toward the right side of the fabric.

4 Edge stitch the outline of the cloud twice with black thread. Sew quickly and allow the lines to overlap and diverge. Backstitch at the beginning and end of the seam.

5 Hand embroider the facial features using backstitches. Use all six strands of black floss for the eyes, and four strands for the nose and mouth. Edge stitch the cheek circles onto the cloud by machine with matching thread.

6 Cut a circle of cotton batting (wadding) a little larger than the hoop, so it is just big enough to wrap around the back edge of the hoop, and then center the batting on the wrong side of the applique fabric. Set aside for the moment.

Keep it Simple
Use a larger embroidery hoop, plates or bowls, or just estimate to make circles larger than the embroidery hoops. The circles do not need to be exact because the edges will be hidden inside the hoops.

To Make the Hoop Back

1 Place the smaller ring of the embroidery hoop onto a piece of chipboard (mountboard). Trace the inner circle onto the board with a pencil. The board circle should be a little smaller than the inside of the hoop, a scant ⅛in (3mm) smaller on all sides, for all hoop sizes. Cut out the circle.

2 Cut one piece of batting (wadding) and one piece of backing fabric into a circle that will fold over the board without overlapping in the middle, as shown.

3 Place the backing fabric right side down, with the batting (wadding) on top. Hand sew a long running stitch around the edge of the circle through both batting and fabric with hand quilting thread. I used dark thread for demonstration, but a neutral color is recommended. Do not tie off the end.

4 Place the board circle in the center of the batting (wadding), hold it down with a finger, and then with the other hand pull the thread in the backing fabric until it gathers up around the board. Securely tie off the thread and trim the end. Sew through all the gathers again, pull the fabric a little tighter so it is smooth and taut but not bending the board, then knot and trim off again. With an iron, press the bunched edges of the fabric and batting all in one direction.

To Assemble

1 Wrap the appliquéd fabric and batting (wadding) around the smaller hoop, then fit the outer hoop over the inner hoop and tighten the screw. Adjust accordingly to ensure the cloud is in the right spot and the fabric is taut.

2 Carefully wrap the appliquéd fabric edges around the back of the inner hoop, and then press the backing, gathered side down, into the hoop. Push the backing until the front of the appliqué fabric bulges out slightly. Hang the hoops with metal wall hangers or anchored screws, or stack some removable adhesive mounting squares on the wall to make a ledge for balancing the hoops.

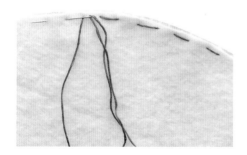

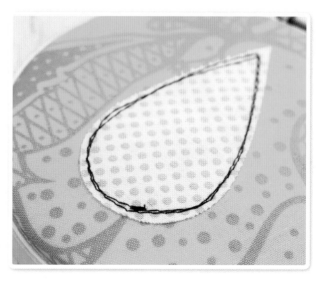

TRAVEL LIGHT

Roll With It Jewelry
WALLET

This pretty patchwork wallet helps keep your favorite sparkly trinkets organized and protected, and is especially handy for travel. Your valuables will stay safe and sound with two zipper pockets and a padded ring holder secured with a shiny pearl snap. The zippers are super easy to sew, with just a hint of a fun coordinating print, and bias tape ties and binding to top it off with a clean finished look.

FINISHED DIMENSIONS:
8in wide x 9½in high (20.5cm x 24cm). All seam allowances ¼in (5mm) unless otherwise stated.

From Your
Scrap Bag

(Cut fabric pieces using the relevant Templates *)

Basic tools
(see Equipment & Materials)

Assorted quilting cotton prints
Thirty 2in (5cm) squares

Three pieces main print for pockets, two 3½in x 8in (9cm x 20.5cm) and one 3in x 8in (7.5cm x 20.5cm)

Three pieces coordinating print for pocket lining, two 3½in x 8in (9cm x 20.5cm) and one 3in x 8in (7.5cm x 20.5cm)

One coordinating print for pocket backing 8in x 9½in (20.5cm x 24cm)

Four 3in x 2in (7.5cm x 5cm) pieces of coordinating print to cover zipper ends

Two ring rolls from template *

1½in x 30in (4cm x 76cm) double-fold tape for ties

2½in x 36in (6.5cm x 1m) single-fold tape for binding

Lightweight fusible interfacing
3in x 8in (7.5cm x 20.5cm)

Pearl snap fastener
No-sew size 16 and snap setting tool

Two 6in (15cm) closed-end zippers

Threads
All-purpose for quilting and piecing, and hand quilting thread for sewing binding

Cotton batting (wadding)
9in x 10½in (23cm x 26.5cm)

Stuffing material

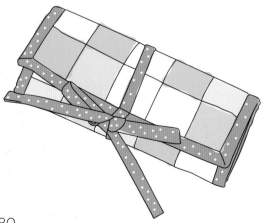

To Make the Patchwork

1 Sew the thirty squares into a rectangle five squares wide by six squares high. Press all seam allowances open.

2 Place the wrong side of the patchwork on top of the batting (wadding) cut slightly larger and quilt as desired. Square up the quilted patchwork and trim to 8in x 9½in (20.5cm x 24cm).

To Make the Ring Roll

1 Attach fusible interfacing to the wrong side of the 3in x 8in (7.5cm x 20.5cm) pocket fabric. Place this piece and the same sized lining piece wrong sides together. Mark a spot centered 1in (2.5cm) from the edge of one of the short sides of the fabric. Attach the stud side of the snap fastener over the mark.

2 Place the two ring roll pieces right sides together and sew around except for the short straight ends. Trim the seam allowance, turn right side out, and press. Attach the pearl side of the snap to the center of the curved end of the ring roll, with the center of the snap about ½in (1.3cm) from the curved edge.

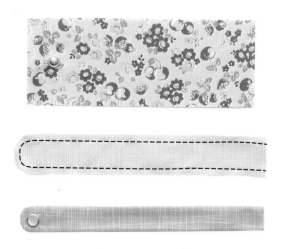

3 Check to make sure your snap works and then fill the ring roll with stuffing material, leaving the last 1in (2.5cm) unstuffed.

Keep it Simple
The blunt end of a chopstick is very handy for stuffing the ring roll.

To Attach the Zippers

1 Unzip both zippers part-way, and then hand sew the open ends together on the center ridged edges between the metal tips and the ends.

2 Press the four 3in x 2in (7.5cm x 5cm) zipper end fabrics in half across the width. Center and topstitch each piece on top of the zippers, with the fold just past the metal ends. Trim the ends of the fabric so the zipper pieces are 8in (20.5cm) long, and the top and bottom of the fabric matches the long edges of the zippers.

3 Place one each of the 3½in x 8in (9cm x 20.5cm) pocket and lining fabric pieces wrong sides together. Place a zipper face down along the top edge of the pocket fabric and pin. When closed, the zipper pull should be on the left side. Using the zipper foot on your machine, sew the zipper to the fabric ¼in (5mm) from the edge. Open or close the zipper pull away from the sewing needle and presser foot as necessary.

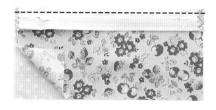

Keep it Simple
This is the perfect project for using the zipper foot on your machine! It lets you sew very close to the zipper without the foot running up over the zipper, or blocking your view.

6 Sew the pocket piece with the snap stud above the zipper, and topstitch, as you did with the previous fabrics. Make sure the stud is on the same side as the closed zipper pull.

7 Sew the remaining zipper onto the top of the snap pocket piece, pocket fabric facing the zipper front. The closed zipper pull should again be on the same side as the snap. Press the fabrics away from the zipper and topstitch.

8 Place the remaining 3½in x 8in (9cm x 20.5cm) pocket and lining pieces wrong sides together and sew to the top of the zipper, with the pocket fabric facing the zipper front. Press the fabrics away from the zipper and topstitch.

To Assemble

1 Square up the assembled zipper section to 8in x 9½in (20.5cm x 24cm), trimming equally on opposite sides as necessary.

2 Place the zipper section on top of the 8in x 9½in (20.5cm x 24cm) pocket backing, right side of backing to the lining side of the zippers. Pin, mark, and triple stitch the pieces together across the center section as shown. Start at the edge and sew as close as possible to the snap stud.

4 Press the fabrics away from the zipper and topstitch along the folded edge.

5 The order that the remaining pieces should be sewn is laid out in the diagram below, bottom to top, and is described in the following steps 6–8.

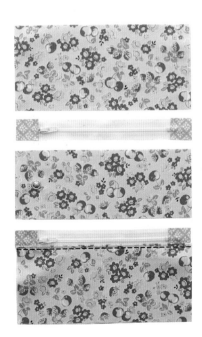

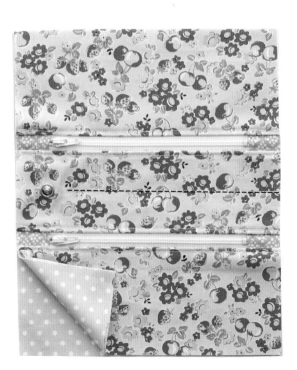

3 Snap together the ring roll to the pocket stud. The raw edge of the roll should hang over the opposite edge of the zipper section. Baste (tack) the short side of the roll in place so the pocket fabric lies flat and does not bunch or stretch. Trim the part of the roll that overhangs the edge.

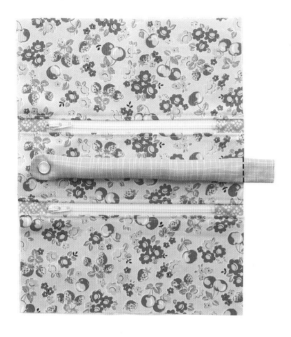

4 Hand stitch closed two pieces of 1½in (4cm) double-fold tape to make the ties using hand quilting thread and ladder stitches, each with one end pressed under ½in (1.3cm). One tie should be cut 11½in (29cm) long, and the other 17in (43cm) long. Stack the raw edges of the two ties with the shorter tie on top, centered on one of the short sides of the patchwork, and baste (tack) in place.

5 Place the patchwork face down, and the zipper section facing up on top of it. Pin together and baste around the edges, keeping the ties out of the way while sewing.

6 Bind the raw edges of the jewelry roll with the 2½in (6.5cm) single-fold tape (see Techniques: Making Binding). Machine stitch the binding to the zipper side of the roll, then hand stitch the binding to the patchwork side (see Techniques: Binding with Mitered Corners). Make sure your ties stay straight and out of the way during the machine sewing.

Sew Perfect

If you can fit your fingernail under the edge of the snap, it is a little too loose. Squeeze the snap in the press from different directions to make sure it is set securely.

Bright as a Button
MAKE-UP POUCH

Cute, curvy zipper pouches are helpful for storing beauty products, school supplies, or other small items. Natural colored linen contrasts with fun cotton prints and matching zippers, and side darts add extra storage inside. Sew on a little twill tape loop and a few small vintage buttons for added personality! Make a set of three pouches, one in each size, for a gorgeous bon voyage gift.

FINISHED DIMENSIONS:

Large 6½in high x 12in wide (16.5cm x 30.5cm); medium 6in x 10½in (15cm x 26.5cm); small 5in x 9in (12.5cm x 23cm). All seam allowances are ¼in (5mm) unless otherwise stated.

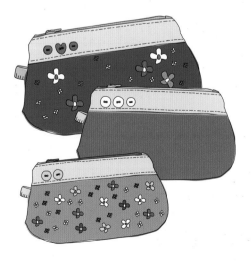

From Your
Scrap Bag

For one bag

(Cut fabric pieces using the relevant Templates *)

Basic tools
(see Equipment & Materials)

Cotton prints
Use appropriate templates for zipper size listed below

Two bag bodies from main print *

Two linings from coordinating print *

Two rectangles, 1in x 2½in (2.5cm x 6.5cm) from another coordinating print

Cotton/linen blend
Two bands *

Lightweight fusible interfacing
Two bag bodies and two bands *

Thread
All-purpose thread to match cotton/linen blend, zipper ends, and lining

One nylon closed-end zipper
For 8in (20.5cm) zipper use Large templates; for 7in (18cm) use Medium templates; for 6in (15cm) use Small templates

Two or three small buttons

Embroidery floss (cotton) for sewing on buttons

Twill tape or ribbon
½in x 2in (1.3cm x 5cm)

To Make the Bag Outer

1 Fuse the same-sized interfacing to the wrong side of the linen and bag body pieces. Place one linen band on a cotton body piece, long straight edges right sides together. Pin and sew together along the long straight edge. Press the linen up and topstitch. Repeat for the other linen and body pieces.

2 Sew the darts on each of the bag outer and lining pieces, as shown. Fold the fabric right sides together, matching the cut-outs, and then triple stitch ¼in (5mm) along the short edge, starting from the raw edges of the fabric and gently curving off the folded edge past the cut-out.

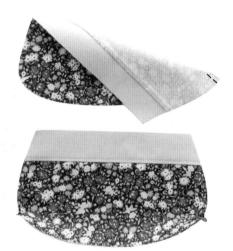

To Add the Zipper and Embellishments

1 Cover the ends of the zipper with the 1in x 2½in (2.5cm x 6.5cm) cotton rectangles. Press the two ends under ¼in (5mm), and then press the entire rectangle in half across the width.

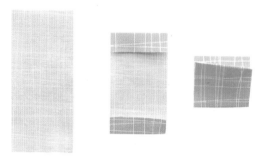

2 Place the end of the zipper inside and topstitch on the fold next to the metal end of the zipper, using the zipper foot on your machine. Repeat for the other side.

3 Unzip the zipper halfway, and then make a 'sandwich' with the bag outer, the zipper, and the lining. Place a bag outer piece right side up. Place the zipper right side (pull side) down, and then a lining piece right side down on top of it and pin, as shown.

4 Sew all the pieces together, beginning ¼in (5mm) from the edge of the fabric and a ¼in (5mm) seam allowance from the long edge. Open or close the zipper pull away from the sewing needle and foot as necessary. Stop ¼in (5mm) from the other side.

5 Press the fabrics away from the zipper and then topstitch on the linen, again, ¼in (5mm) from the edges. Slightly pull the fabrics away from the zipper as you sew. Repeat steps 3–4 above for the other outer and lining pieces.

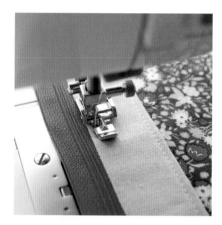

6 Close the zipper. Fold a piece of twill tape or ribbon and sew onto only the bag front on the same side as the zipper pull, raw edges of the tape and bag together, just below the band. Baste (tack) close to the edge.

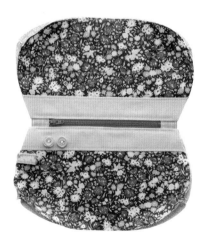

7 Sew the buttons to the linen band with embroidery floss.

To Finish

1 Open the zipper about three-quarters of the way – this is *very* important, as it will allow you to turn the bag right side out after sewing it together. Open up the fabrics so the bag outer pieces are right sides together, and the bag lining pieces are right sides together.

2 Fold the ends of the zipper in half *toward* the lining, and help the lining fabric pleat neatly on top and below it. The fabric should comfortably fold right at the topstitching underneath. Use a binding clip to hold all the layers together. Match all the other sides and pin, taking special care to match the linen seams on the bag outer and the darts on all the pieces.

3 Sew all the way around the bag, *except* for a 2in–3in (5cm–7.5cm) hole on one side of the lining, a few stitches above the dart.

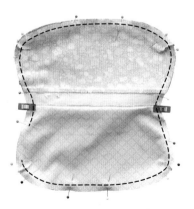

4 Trim the curved seam allowances, and turn the bag right side out through the hole. Carefully tuck in and press the unsewn lining, and sew it closed with matching thread, very close to the edge. Put the lining back in the bag to finish.

Down to Business
CARD HOLDER

This little card holder is one of my favorite on-the-go accessories. It can be used to carry business cards, or as a small wallet, comfortably fitting an ID, credit cards, and cash. Two pearl snaps help keep everything in place. The card holder matches the Craft-on-the-Go Tote Bag, with a linen flap and coordinating fabric prints on the inside, but you can make yours to go with any bag or outfit.

FINISHED DIMENSIONS:
3½in high x 4¼in wide (9cm x 11cm). All seam allowances are ¼in (5mm) unless otherwise stated.

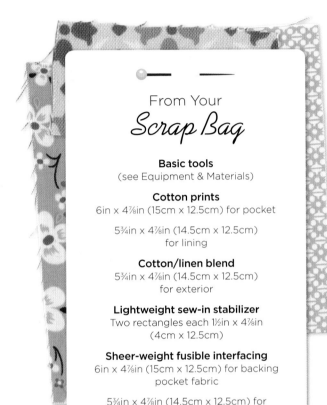

From Your
Scrap Bag

Basic tools
(see Equipment & Materials)

Cotton prints
6in x 4⅞in (15cm x 12.5cm) for pocket

5¾in x 4⅞in (14.5cm x 12.5cm) for lining

Cotton/linen blend
5¾in x 4⅞in (14.5cm x 12.5cm) for exterior

Lightweight sew-in stabilizer
Two rectangles each 1½in x 4⅞in (4cm x 12.5cm)

Sheer-weight fusible interfacing
6in x 4⅞in (15cm x 12.5cm) for backing pocket fabric

5¾in x 4⅞in (14.5cm x 12.5cm) for backing linen

Threads
All-purpose thread for inside of holder, and hand quilting thread in a neutral color

Two pearl snaps
No-sew size 16 and snap setting tool

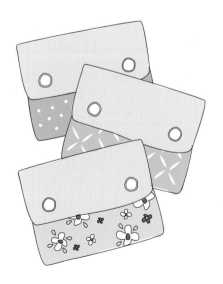

To Make the Pocket

1 Attach same-sized fusible interfacing to the wrong side of the pocket fabric. Press the pocket fabric across the width, wrong sides together, so it measures 3in x 4⅞in (7.5cm x 12.5cm). Unfold the fabric and place right side down.

2 Place one of the stabilizer rectangles just under the fold, and then baste (tack) in place along each of the short sides.

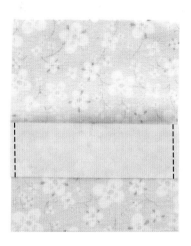

To Assemble

1 Attach same-sized fusible interfacing to the wrong side of the linen.

2 Place the lining fabric right side up, and then place the pocket on top, raw edges matching on the sides and bottom of the lining. Baste (tack) in place along the sides, as shown.

3 Mark the front of the pocket with two dots for the snap placement, each ¾in (2cm) away from the fold over the side with the stabilizer, and 1in (2.5cm) away from the raw edges.

4 Attach stud snaps centered over each of the dots, through *only* the layer of fabric with the stabilizer underneath. The studs should be on the right side of the fabric. Re-fold the pocket over the back of the studs and press along the fold.

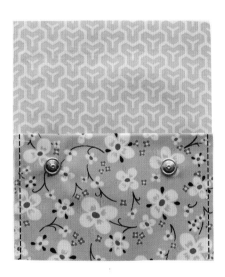

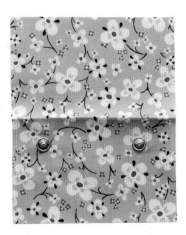

3 Place the linen on top, right side facing down, with the remaining stabilizer rectangle across the top edge. Pin in place on the top edge.

5 Triple stitch around the edge of the holder, leaving a 2in (5cm) hole on one side for turning. Make sure to sew through the top edge of the pocket, and sew a few stitches before turning the bottom corner.

4 Use a thread spool or one of the small circle templates from the book (such as the owl eyes) to trace and trim just the top edges of the linen and lining fabrics.

6 Trim the corners and seam allowances, except around the turning hole, then turn right side out and press.

7 Mark the flap with placement dots for the pearl snaps on the outside of the flap, each ¾in (2cm) from the long sides and ½in (1.3cm) from the top. The pearl part of the snaps should be on the linen.

8 Sew the turning hole closed with hand quilting thread and ladder stitch. Fold over the flap and close the snaps, and then crease the fold in the flap with an iron to finish.

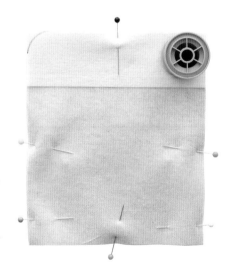

Take It Easy
CROSS-BODY BAG

A cute cross-body bag is so convenient for hands-free shopping – just throw in the necessities and go! This little bag has a zippered pocket on the back, divided slip pocket in the main compartment, and the flap is secured with a magnetic snap. The front and inside pocket are made with remnants of cotton prints, the lining is a solid color, and colorfully quilted Essex yarn-dyed linen is used for the back, strap, and flap.

FINISHED DIMENSIONS:
7½in high x 9¾in wide (19cm x 25cm) excluding straps (see Chic Scrap Style overleaf). All seam allowances are ¼in (5mm) unless otherwise stated.

From Your
Scrap Bag

(Cut fabric pieces using the relevant Templates)

Basic tools
(see Equipment & Materials)

Cotton prints
9in x 11in (23cm x 28cm) for bag front

12in x 11in (30.5cm x 28cm) for inside pocket

Solid cotton
One fat quarter or ½yd (0.5m) for lining

Yarn-dyed Essex linen or cotton/ linen blend
1½yd (1.4m) if single piece strap, or ¾yd (0.75m) if strap will be pieced

Fusible fleece ½yd (0.5m)

Sheer-weight fusible interfacing ¾yd (0.75m)

All-purpose threads
In various colors for quilting, assembly, and topstitching

Closed-end zipper 8in (20.5cm)

Magnetic snap fastener ¾in (2cm) diameter

Ultra-firm interfacing (Peltex)
For backing snaps

To Cut the Bag Pieces

1 Use the templates provided where needed, and cut the following pieces of fabric.

- Cut three bag bodies from solid cotton lining fabric.

- Cut one lower bag body and one upper bag body piece from solid cotton lining fabric.

- Cut one flap from solid cotton lining fabric and back it with same-sized lightweight fusible interfacing.

- Cut Essex linen 10in x 12in (25.5cm x 30.5cm) for the back of the bag. Attach fusible fleece to the wrong side.

- Cut Essex linen 6in x 10in (15cm x 25.5cm) for flap. Attach same-sized fusible fleece to the wrong side.

- Cut two pieces of Essex linen, each 1in x 3in (2.5cm x 7.5cm) for zipper ends.

- Cut Essex linen 4in x 49in (10cm x 124.5cm) for the strap. If necessary, piece together two strips 4in x 24¾in (10cm x 63cm) to make the full length. Cut two strips of fusible interfacing 1⅞in x 24½in (5cm x 62cm) and fuse to the wrong side of the strap fabric along the center.

- Cut one bag body from a cotton print for front of bag. Attach same-sized fusible fleece to the wrong side.

- Cut two ovals from ultra-firm interfacing a little larger than the snap pieces will be (with the prongs bent outward).

Chic Scrap Style

For a customized strap length, measure from your hip, over the opposite shoulder and back to your hip with a loose tape measure. Add 1in (2.5cm) to the length for seam allowances.

To Quilt the Back, Flap, and Strap

1 Quilt the Essex linen squares for the back and flap with various thread colors that coordinate with the bag front print. Mark a few random vertical and horizontal lines with a disappearing ink fabric pen and quilt the colors one at a time.

2 Fold the larger square across the width and cut one lower bag body piece and one upper body piece by placing the template arrows on the fold and cutting with a rotary cutter. Cut one flap from the quilted flap fabric in the same way.

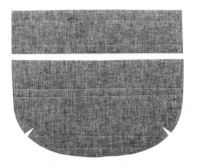

3 Quilt the strap fabric by sewing random short lines across the width with various thread colors (the underside is shown in the diagram). Press the strap as you would double-fold tape (see Techniques: Making Binding) and topstitch each long side with any color desired.

Sew Perfect

Use a size 14 Sharps needle for all topstitching as the larger gauge needle goes through multiple layers of fabric easily and yields more consistent stitches.

To Make the Zipper Pocket

1 Cover the ends of the zipper with the 1in x 3in (2.5cm x 7.5cm) Essex linen rectangles (see Make-Up Pouch, To Add the Zipper and Embellishments, diagrams with steps 1 and 2). The ends of the zipper will not go all the way to the fold.

2 Unzip the zipper about halfway, then make a sandwich with the linen lower bag body, zipper, and solid cotton lower bag body pieces, matching all long straight edges. Place the linen right side up, the zipper right side (pull side) down, and the solid cotton right side down on top of it and pin. The zipper pull will be on the left side when closed.

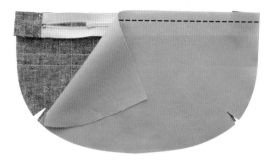

3 Using the zipper foot, sew all the pieces together with a ¼in (5mm) seam allowance, all the way across the long edge. Open or close the zipper pull away from the sewing needle and presser foot as necessary.

4 Press the lining and linen away from the zipper, and then topstitch over the original seam. Slightly pull the fabrics away from the zipper as you sew.

5 Repeat steps 3 and 4 for the linen and solid cotton upper bag body pieces for the top edge of the zipper. Remember to match the plaid quilting lines on the top and bottom pieces.

To Make the Inside Pocket

1 Fold the pocket fabric across the width and wrong sides together so it remains 11in (28cm) wide. Place the lower bag body template on the left side of the fabric with the pocket line matching the fold. Trace around the curved edge, then turn over the template at the midpoint and continue tracing to finish the curve. Cut on the traced line. Do the same with a piece of sheer-weight fusible interfacing. Attach the interfacing to the wrong side of the pocket fabric. Re-fold and press the pocket in half across the width, wrong sides together.

2 Place the pocket onto one of the solid cotton bag bodies, right sides together and pin. Make sure the pocket top is level with the top of the body piece, and then baste (tack) in place around the raw edges. Triple stitch the pocket dividers as desired.

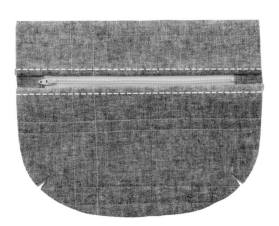

2 Insert the socket side of the snap through the right side of the printed bag body according to the template marking (as you did in step 1 above).

To Make the Flap

1 Mark and cut notches in the solid flap fabric for inserting the snap, according to the template marking. Insert the stud side of the magnetic snap through the right side of the solid flap, through an interfacing oval on the wrong side of the fabric, and then place the washer over the prongs, as shown. Place something soft between your surface and the snap when bending the prongs. The handle of a heavy screwdriver is handy for bending the prongs outward.

3 Place the linen and cotton flap pieces right sides together, pin, and sew around the curve only. Trim the seam allowance, turn right side out, press carefully, and topstitch around the curve. It is helpful to pin a piece of fabric over the snap to prevent scuffs while topstitching – just make sure the pins and fabric edges stay clear of the seam allowances.

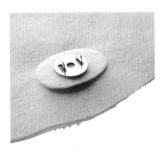

To Assemble the Bag

1 Place the zipper pocket section on top of one of the lining bodies and pin right sides together. This will function as one body piece.

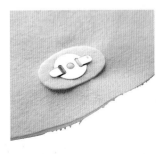

2 Sew the darts on all of the bag bodies (the bag back with the zipper, the bag front, and two lining pieces) by folding the fabric right sides together and stitching a ¼in (5mm) seam that curves around the notch to the folded edge (see Make-Up Pouch, To Make the Bag Outer, diagram with step 2). For pieces with multiple layers, fold all the layers together.

3 Place the zipper body section and the printed body section right sides together, and then pin and triple stitch all the way around the curve (see top part of diagram, below). Trim the seam allowances except for the top 1in (2.5cm) on each side and turn right side out. This is the bag outer.

4 Place the two remaining bag bodies (one with the divided pocket, one without) right sides together. Match the darts, pin, and triple stitch together around the curved edges, except for a 3in (7.5cm) hole above one of the darts for turning (see lower part of diagram). This is the bag lining.

5 Place the flap on the zipper side of the bag outer, linen sides together. Center and pin the flap, and then baste (tack) in place, as shown.

6 Center the raw ends of the strap over the side seams on the right side of the bag outer and securely sew in place close to the edge. Make sure the strap is not twisted.

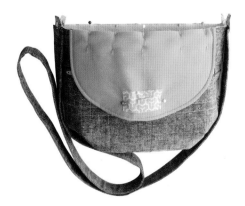

7 Turn the bag outer inside out and fold up the strap in the bottom of the bag. Turn the bag lining right side out and place inside the bag outer, right sides together. Match up the side seams and use binding clips to secure the two pieces together on the side seams. Pin the rest of the way around the bag, making sure there are no wrinkles or folds along the top edge. Triple stitch all the way around the top of the bag.

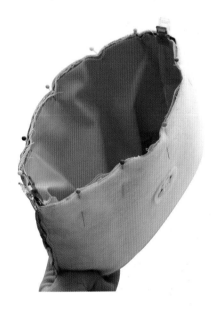

8 Turn the bag right side out through the hole in the lining. Press the lining hole edges under and sew closed. Press the top of the bag, making sure the lining is not visible on the outside. To finish, topstitch around the top of the bag using thread that matches the front of the bag.

TECHNIQUES

This section describes and illustrates the general techniques you will need for the projects in the book.

Preparing Fabric

The right side of the fabric is the side on which the pattern is printed, or the more textured side of linen fabric. The wrong side of the fabric is not printed, or the smoother side of linen fabric. Some people like to wash their fabrics before use, while others don't, preferring the slightly crinkled look of patchwork that has shrunk a little in the wash. Press all fabric before use to remove creases and make cutting more accurate. Trim off the selvages – these are the lengthwise edges of the fabric that have either a woven or frayed edge, with holes along the side.

Pressing

When pressing with an iron, make sure that you *press*, not iron, that is, move the iron around the fabric. Place the iron on the spot you want to press, and use the weight of the iron and a little pressure or steam to do the pressing. To press a new area, lift the iron and place it on the new spot. Gliding the iron around will warp the fabric and make your patchwork less accurate.

Seam Allowances

A seam allowance is the distance between the raw edge of the fabric and the seam. For patchwork piecing this is normally ¼in (5mm), and maintaining an accurate seam allowance will help your patches fit together neatly. Seams can be pressed open, or to one side – follow the project instructions.

Sewing Patchwork Pieces

The patchwork in this book uses straight seams to sew fabric strips, squares, or rectangles together. To join pieces, cut your pieces accurately and then place them right sides together. Sew a ¼in (5mm) seam and press the seam allowance.

To join squares together in rows, press the seams of the first row in one direction and the seams of the second row in the opposite direction, and so on. Then when you come to sew the rows together it will be easier to align or nest the seams neatly.

Sewing Curves

For sewing tight curves by machine, I recommend sewing one or two stitches, and then, leaving the needle in the down position, lift the presser foot and turn your project slightly. Lower the presser foot, sew another stitch or two and then make another slight turn as before. Continue until you have sewn all the way around the turn.

Machine Stitches

The projects use stitches found on most sewing machines.

Backstitch

A couple of extra stitches should be worked back and forth at the beginning and end of a seam to prevent thread from unraveling. Always backstitch seams unless otherwise directed.

Baste/Machine Baste

Basting (tacking) is a long straight stitch used to temporarily hold fabric in place, typically sewn very close to the raw edge of the fabric, less than ¼in (5mm).

Edge Stitch

This is a seam sewn close to the edge of the fabric, typically ⅛in (3mm) or less from the edge, with a normal stitch length.

Straight Stitch

This is a standard machine stitch used to sew pieces of fabric together, and can also be used for machine quilting.

Topstitching

This is a straight stich sewn very close to an edge, such as around the top of a bag, which adds a finishing touch and secures the seam allowances underneath. Use a stitch length slightly longer than normal, and if necessary, a heavier duty needle when sewing through several layers of fabric.

Triple Stitch

Triple stitch is a machine stitch reinforced with two extra stitches, used to sew a seam. Most machines are equipped with this stitch – check your user manual to find out where the button or setting is on your machine. If your machine does not have a triple stitch, sew a regular straight stitch, and then sew over it two more times to reinforce the seam.

Hand Stitches

Simple hand stitches are used on some of the projects to sew parts of projects together or to add decoration.

Backstitch

Hand backstitch resembles a machine straight stitch. The needle comes up ahead of where you want to sew the stitch and goes back down into the hole of the previous stitch.

Satin Stitch

Satin stitches are long stitches sewn very close together to create a smooth, satiny surface. They were used for the eyes on the Sweet Sailor Dress Doll.

Whip Stitch

This is a stitch used to wrap around the edge of the fabric, to secure it or add a decorative edging.

Running Stitch

These are straight stitches sewn with a space between each one. It is created by weaving the needle up and down through the fabric. This style of stitch can also be used for hand quilting.

Ladder Stitch

This is a series of parallel stitches used for closing holes or finishing binding, which looks like a ladder until the thread is pulled tight. I finish binding by hand with ladder stitches because I think it gives a cleaner look than machine sewing, and doesn't leave a loose edge that curls up after washing.

Appliqué

Appliqué is a decorative technique of attaching one piece of fabric on top of another. For the appliqué projects in this book, you will need paper-backed fusible web, which is an adhesive material with a removable paper backing. It is sold off the bolt in fabric stores or in pre-packaged quantities. The instructions below outline how to use fusible web to cut and attach appliqués to fabric.

1 Cut a piece of fusible web that is slightly larger than the size of the template, and place it adhesive (rough) side to the wrong side of the fabric. Press on top of the paper with a hot iron (unless the package instructions say otherwise), and then wait until the fabric is completely cooled.

2 Lift the corner of the paper and peel it about one-third of the way off the fabric, then put it back in place (see photo A). This makes it easier to remove the paper after you've cut out the appliqué.

3 Trace around the template onto the paper backing with an extra-fine permanent marker (B). If the shape being copied is asymmetrical you will need to reverse (flip) the template over before you trace, so the shape will appear the right way around on the finished project.

4 Cut around your traced line and then remove the paper (C). Place the sticky side of the appliqué onto the right side of the background fabric and press with an iron to fuse it in place.

5 Stitch around the appliqué with a zigzag stitch (to encase the raw edge) or straight stitch (to leave the edge raw), as directed in the project instructions.

Backstitch

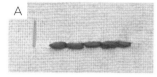

Satin stitch

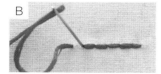

Appliqué

Whip stitch

Running stitch

Ladder stitch

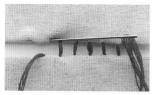

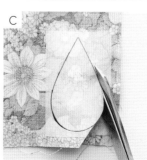

2
Now center the wrong side of the pressed patchwork on top of the batting (wadding).

3
Make sure all layers are smooth and straight, and then pin all the layers together with quilter's safety pins for large projects or regular straight pins for smaller projects.

Stuffing Projects

Some of the projects need stuffing to make them three-dimensional, such as the Pajama Bears and the Owl Bookends. Projects take more stuffing than you expect! Fill the item until it is pretty firm, but not so much that the seams are stretching.

1
Use small tufts of stuffing material and start by filling in the part of the project furthest away from the stuffing hole, and then work your way toward the hole.

2
Make sure ears have stuffing all the way to the tips, and that necks are firm with enough stuffing to support the head. Use the blunt end of a chopstick or stuffing tool to push stuffing into little nooks and those last little hollow spots.

3
Continue to add stuffing when closing the last seam with ladder stitches. Sew a couple of stiches, and then use the chopstick to push stuffing under the newly closed area. Continue this way until you can no longer fit the chopstick into the hole.

Quilt Sandwich

A quilt sandwich is the term used to describe the three layers of a quilt – the top, the batting (wadding), and the backing.

1
Place your pressed backing fabric right side down, smoothing it out. Center the batting (wadding) on top of it, again making sure it is smoothed it out.

Quilting

When quilting by machine, I use a stitch that is slightly longer than usual, a length of 3.5 to 4.0. Use a walking foot on your machine for quilting projects with batting (wadding). The stitches may be sewn in a straight line in regular distances away from seams, to echo the pattern of the patchwork, or directly between pieced fabrics (called 'in the ditch' quilting).

Squaring Up

This is a term used to describe trimming all the edges and corners of a quilt or project to remove excess material and make it regular in shape. This is normally done just before binding, using a large quilter's square and/or ruler and rotary cutter.

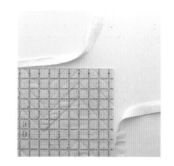

Preparing Bias-Cut Strips for Binding

Single-fold and double-fold bindings are used for some of the projects. The instructions for each project will specify whether the binding should be cut on the bias, as described below, or not. A rule of thumb is that if the project has curves, cut strips on the bias, but if it is square, cut your strips perpendicular to the selvage.

1 To cut strips for bias tape, place a quilting ruler with the 45-degree line along the fabric selvage, and cut along the top edge of the ruler with a rotary cutter (see photo A). Cut strips the width directed in the instructions.

2 Trim the angled ends of the bias tape so the corners are straight and square (B).

3 To join bias-cut strips, place two strips with the short ends right sides together at a right angle. Sew a diagonal seam from the upper left corner of the top strip to the lower right corner as shown (C). Trim the seam allowances and press open.

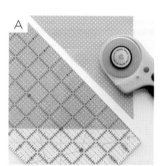

A

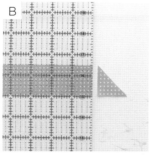

C

Making Binding

My methods of making single-fold and double-fold bindings create firm and neat edgings, but are a little different from the standard methods you may be familiar with.

Single-Fold Binding

If make single-fold binding, prepare your binding strip length as described above. Press the bias tape in half all along the length, wrong sides together.

Double-Fold Binding

If making double-fold binding, prepare your binding strip length as described above. Press the bias tape in half lengthwise. Open up the fabric and press the long sides of the tape toward the center, with the edges not quite touching. Fold the bias tape along the original central crease and press a third time.

Binding with Mitered Corners

When binding square projects such as quilts, the binding fabric does not need to be cut on the bias. The square projects in this book join binding tape with straight seams, however if you prefer to join strips at a 45-degree angle, such as when using a single color of fabric, see Preparing Bias-Cut Strips for Binding.

Attaching Single-Fold Binding

1 Attach the raw edge of the binding along the raw edge of the project with binding clips (see photo A on page 104). Leaving a 6in–8in (15cm–20.5cm) tail unsewn, sew the binding to the quilt ⅜in (1cm) from the edge, and then stop and backstitch ⅜in (1cm) before reaching the first corner. Remove the quilt from the machine and trim the threads.

2 Fold the binding away from the quilt at a 90-degree angle and hold in place at the miter corner (B).

3 Re-fold the binding down to match up with the next side of your quilt. The new fold should exactly match the edge of the quilt. Use binding clips to hold it in place.

4 Starting ⅜in (1cm) from the top edge of the quilt, backstitch and sew the binding to your quilt with the same ⅜in (1cm) seam allowance as before (C). Repeat sewing and turning the remaining three corners in this manner until you are about 15in (38cm) away from the beginning of the seam, and the two binding ends overlap by a few inches. Backstitch, trim the threads, and remove the quilt from the machine.

5 To connect the binding, overlap the two loose ends (D). Mark and trim the binding so it overlaps by 1in (2.5cm). If binding a single color, you may prefer to attach the binding at a 45-degree angle (see also Binding Curves, below).

6 Open both ends of the binding, match the short ends and place the right sides together – make sure the binding will not be twisted and will fold flat once sewn – and stitch them together with a ½in (1.3cm) seam allowance (E). Press the seam allowance open, re-fold the binding and press the crease. Finish sewing the last several inches of binding in place.

7 Fold over the edge of the binding, so the fold of the binding just covers the seam on the back, and sew in place all around by hand with a ladder stitch.

8 When folding over corners, make sure the binding on the front stays folded neatly, then wrap the binding over the corner and overlap the fabric at a 45-degree angle. Sew the corners in place with ladder stitches on the front and back.

Binding Curves

Binding a curved edge requires the binding to be cut on the bias – see Preparing Bias-Cut Strips for Binding. Cut and press the binding to the width and length as directed in the project instructions.

1 Attach the raw edge of the bias binding along the raw edge of the project with binding clips (unfolded if double-fold tape, folded if single-fold tape) – see photo A. Allow the binding ends to overlap a few inches. Mark the bottom strip with a disappearing ink fabric pen where the top strip overlaps.

2 Fully unfold the binding tape and place it right sides together. The top end should lie at a 90-degree angle just to the left of the mark. Make sure the binding will not be twisted once it is sewn together. Sew a diagonal seam, starting at the lower corner opposite the mark, up to the opposite top corner (B). Trim the seam allowance and press it open.

3 Re-fold and press the binding. Re-attach the binding with clips as you did in step 1, unfolding it if necessary (C). Sew along the crease closest to the raw edge if using double-fold tape. Sew as directed if using single-fold tape.

4 Fold the binding over the edge of the project and finish sewing it in place by hand with a ladder stitch.

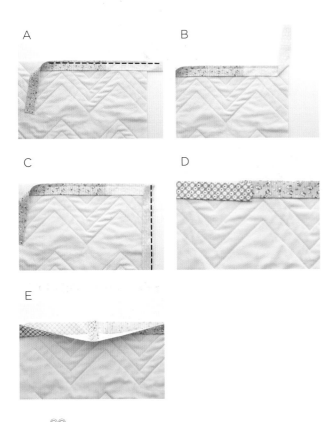

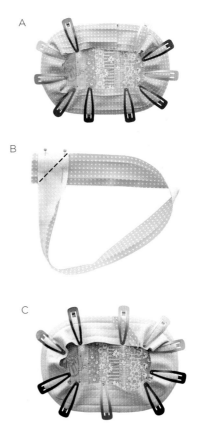

A

B

C

TEMPLATES

The project templates are found in this section, generally following the book order. The templates are actual size and seam allowances are included, so there is no need to enlarge them. A 1in red square is shown on the template pages to denote actual-size scaling. Templates with arrows that point toward the edge are intended to be placed on the fabric fold, as in this case the template is half size. Straight edges of the templates should be positioned either parallel or perpendicular to the fabric selvage. Position the templates consistently for multiple pieces cut from the same fabric print.

If you wish to print these templates out before cutting, you can download a printable PDF from http://ideas.stitchcraftcreate.co.uk/patterns

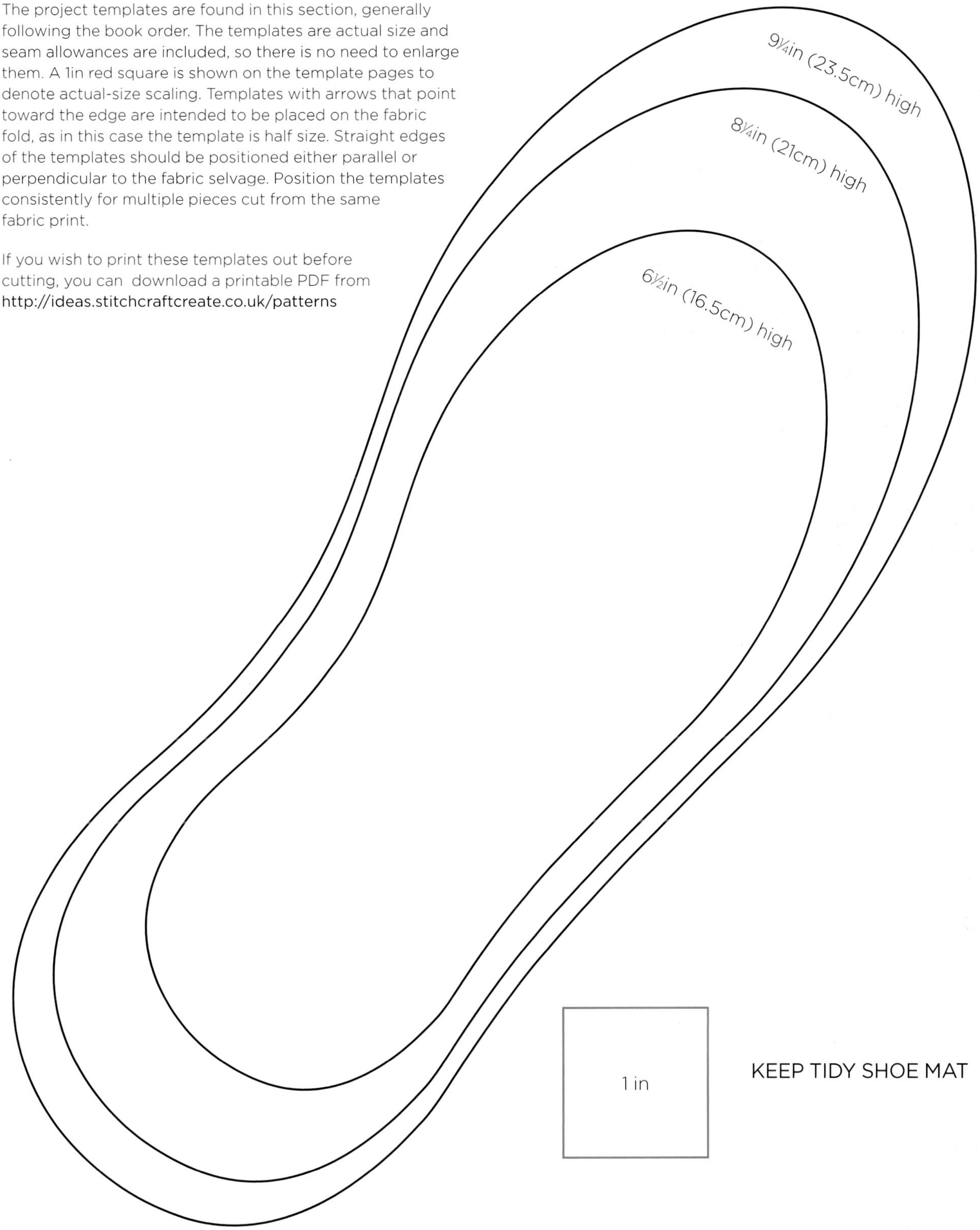

9¼in (23.5cm) high

8¼in (21cm) high

6½in (16.5cm) high

1 in

KEEP TIDY SHOE MAT

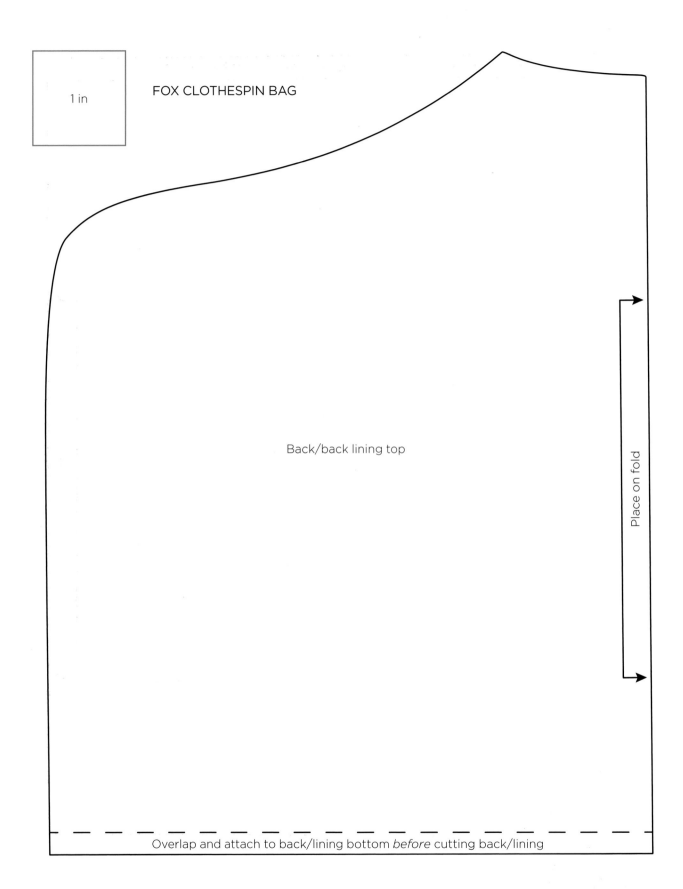

1 in

FOX CLOTHESPIN BAG

Back/back lining top

Place on fold

Overlap and attach to back/lining bottom *before* cutting back/lining

TEMPLATES

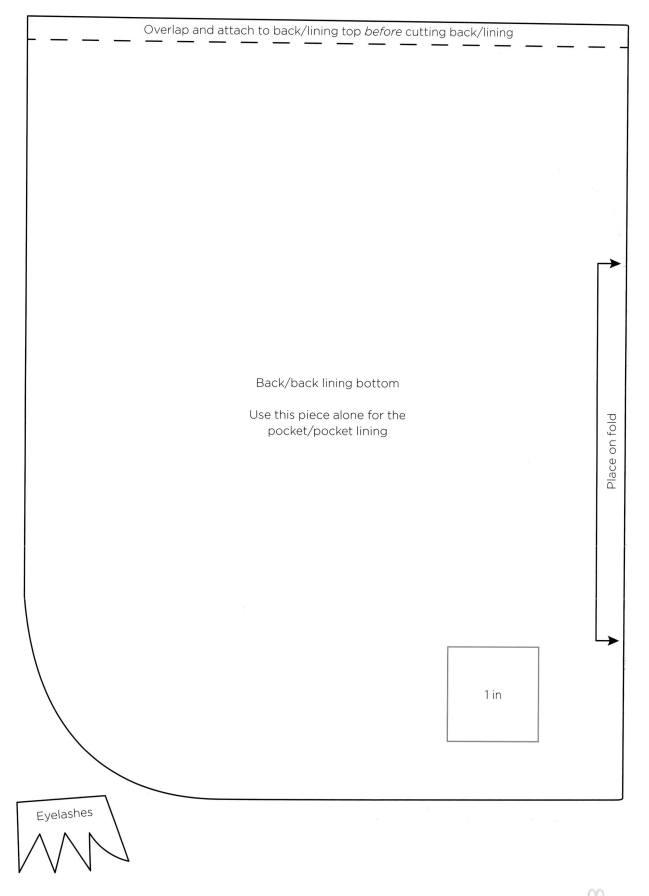

Overlap and attach to back/lining top *before* cutting back/lining

Back/back lining bottom

Use this piece alone for the pocket/pocket lining

Place on fold

1 in

Eyelashes

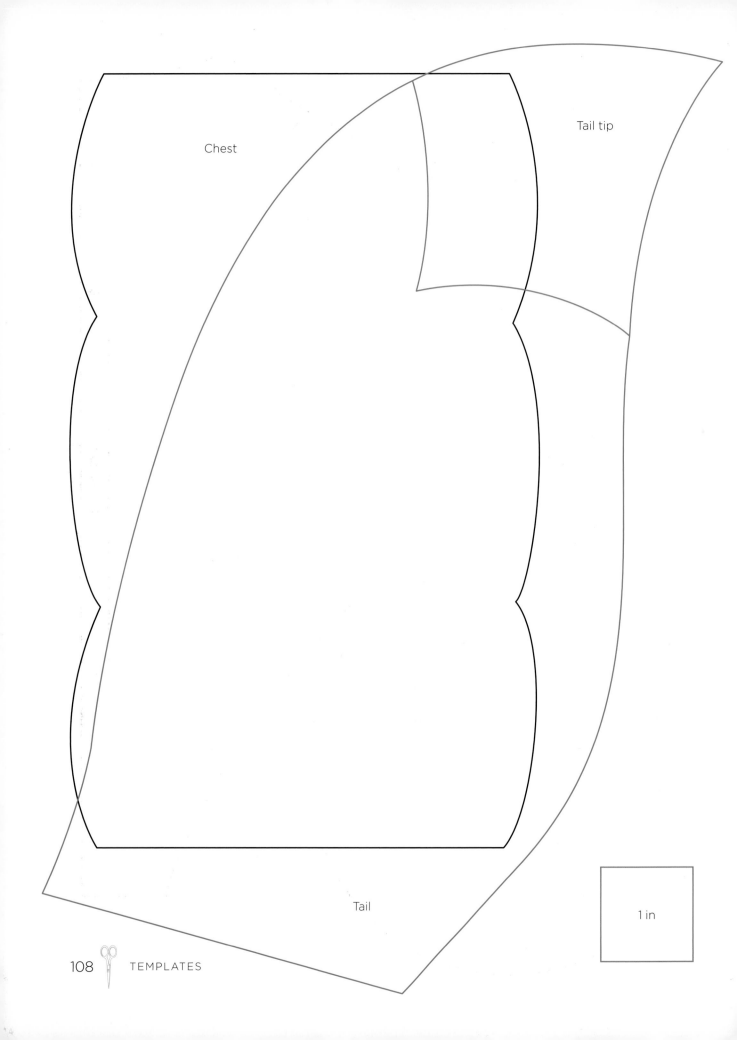

Chest

Tail tip

Tail

1 in

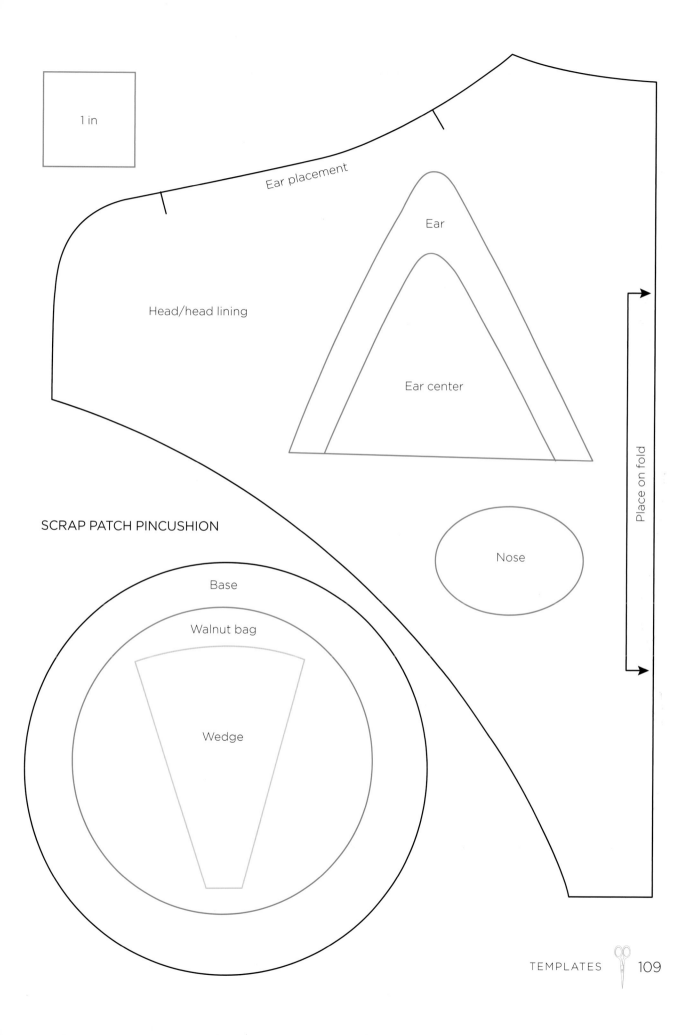

1 in

Ear placement

Head/head lining

Ear

Ear center

Place on fold

SCRAP PATCH PINCUSHION

Nose

Base

Walnut bag

Wedge

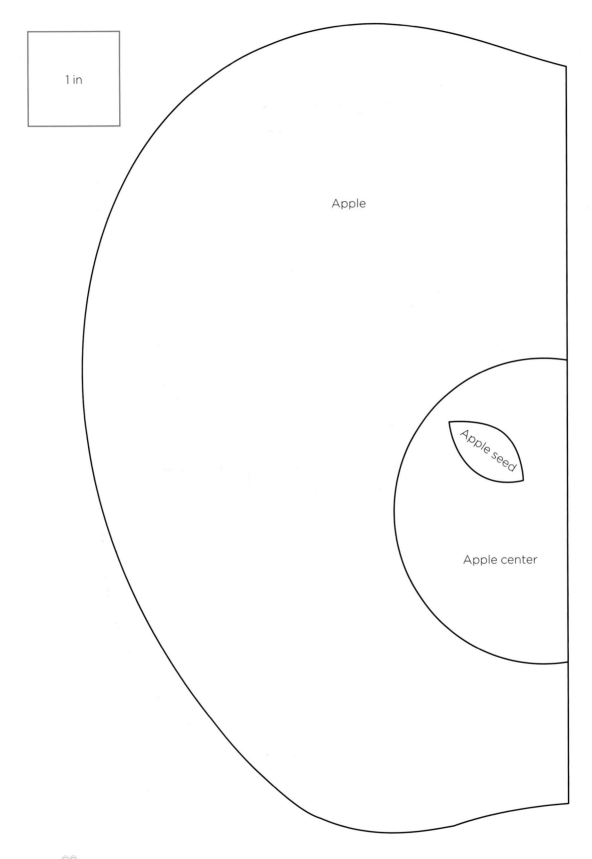

1 in

Apple

Apple seed

Apple center

SIMPLY STRIPPY SEWING KIT

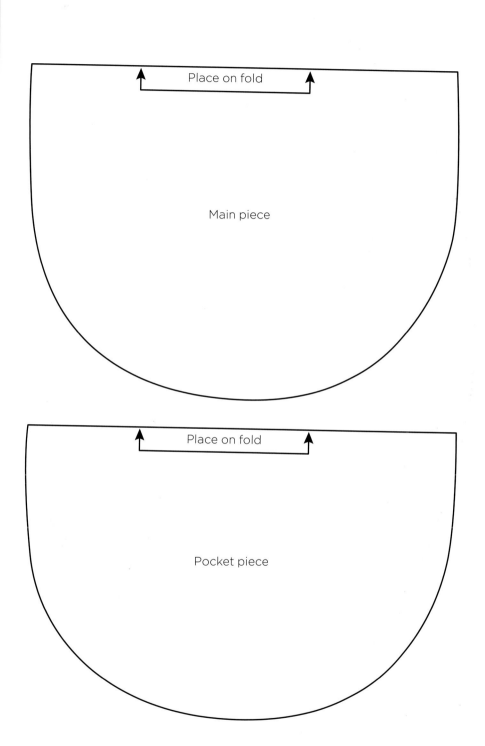

1 in

Place on fold

Main piece

Place on fold

Pocket piece

ON A ROLL CROCHET HOOK HOLDER

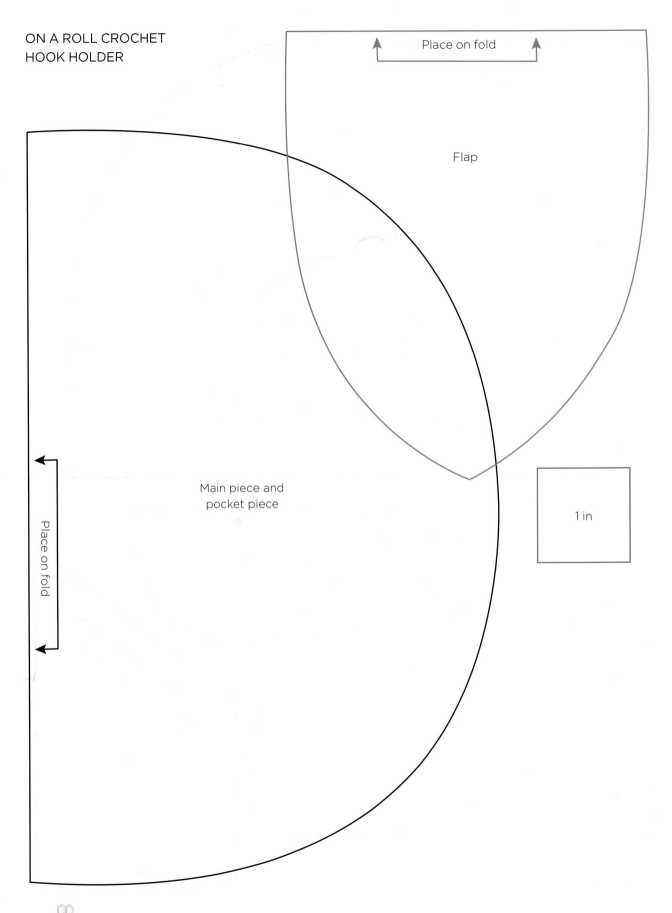

Place on fold

Flap

Main piece and
pocket piece

Place on fold

1 in

PAJAMA BEAR SOFTIES

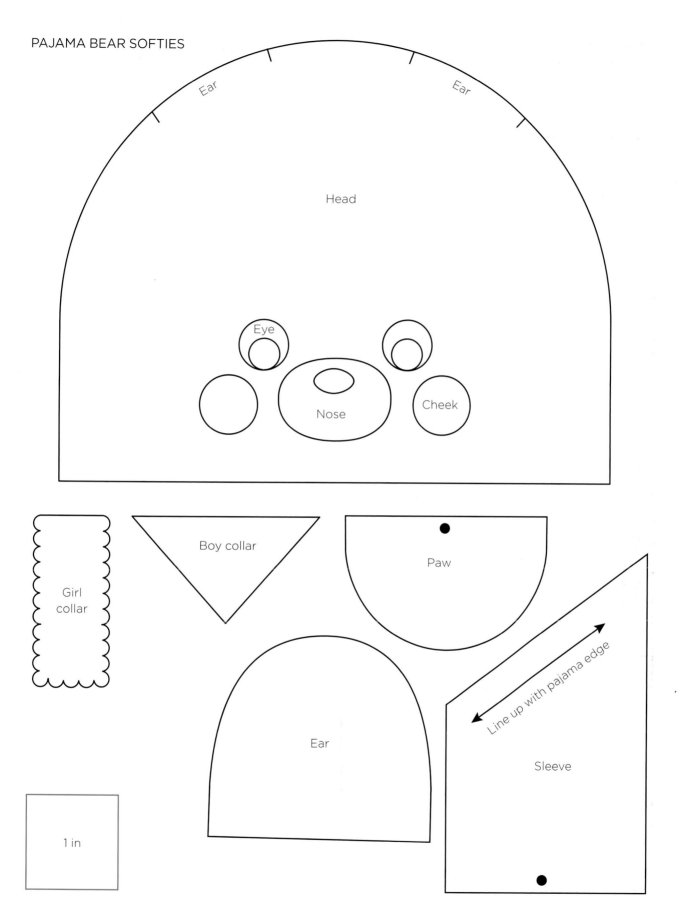

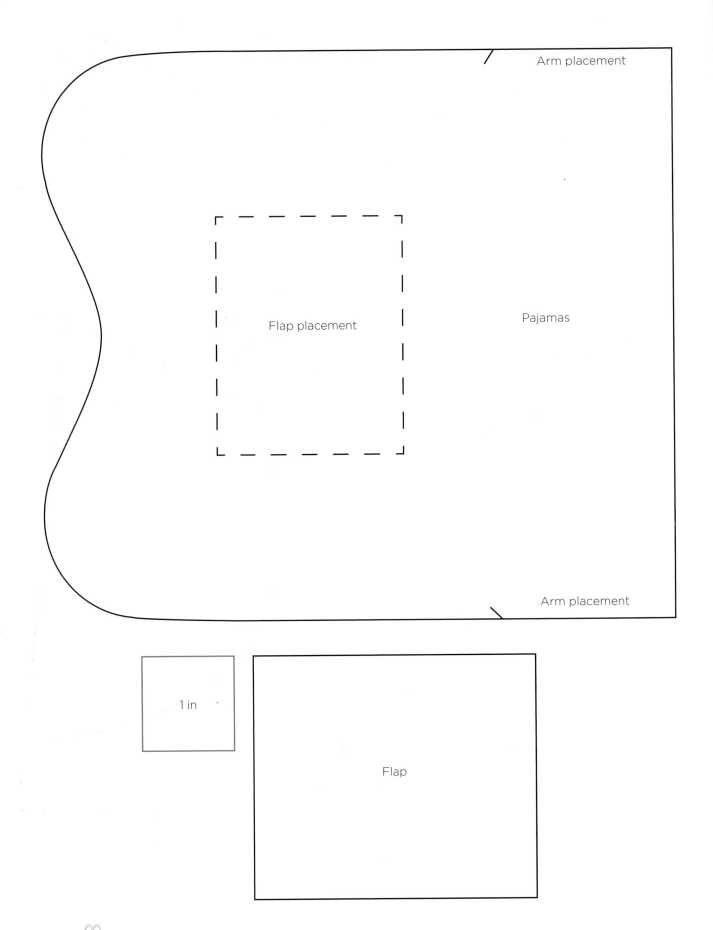

Arm placement

Flap placement

Pajamas

Arm placement

1 in

Flap

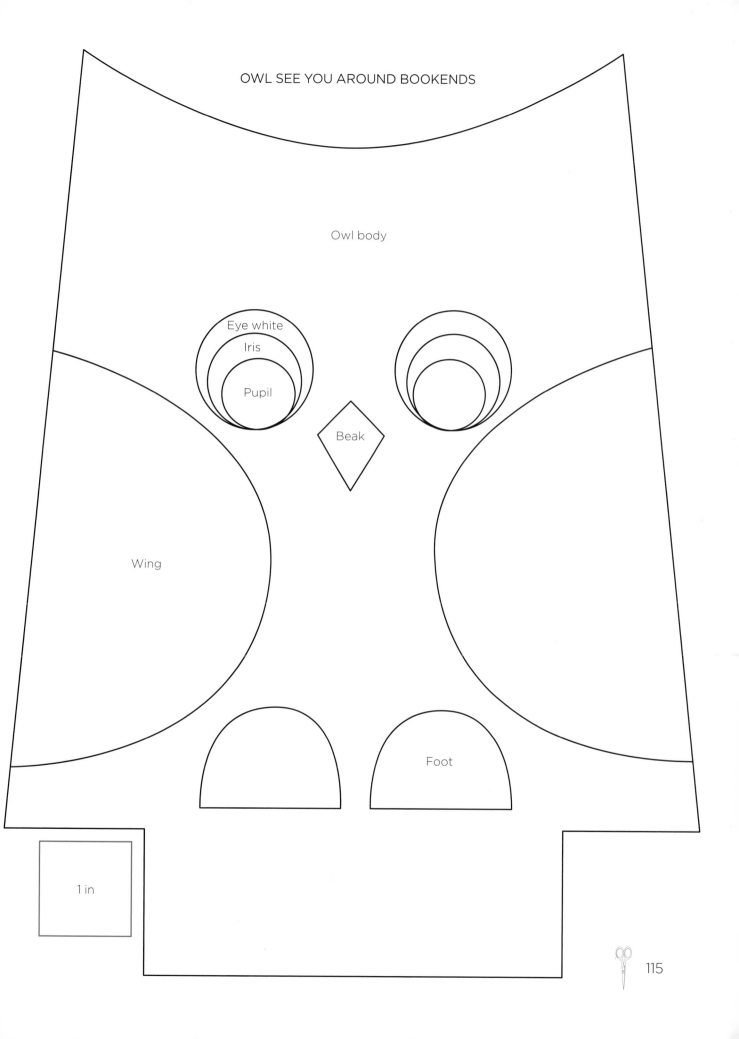

OWL SEE YOU AROUND BOOKENDS

Owl body

Eye white

Iris

Pupil

Beak

Wing

Foot

1 in

115

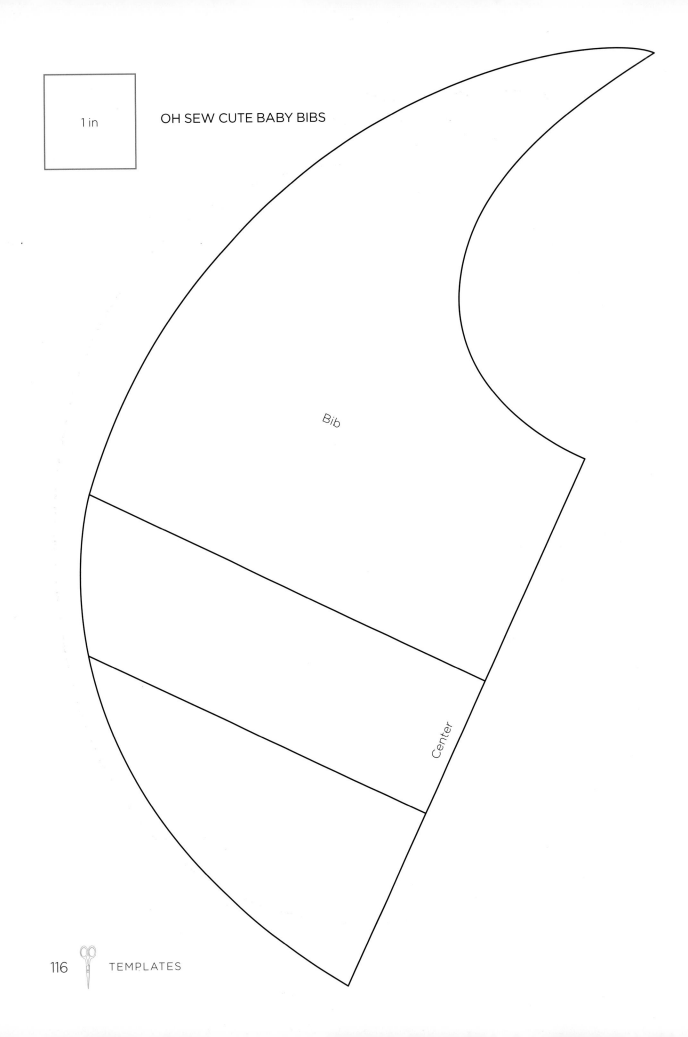

1 in

OH SEW CUTE BABY BIBS

Bib

Center

SWEET SAILOR DRESS DOLL

Stitch the facial features as described
in the project instructions

Head

1 in

Hair

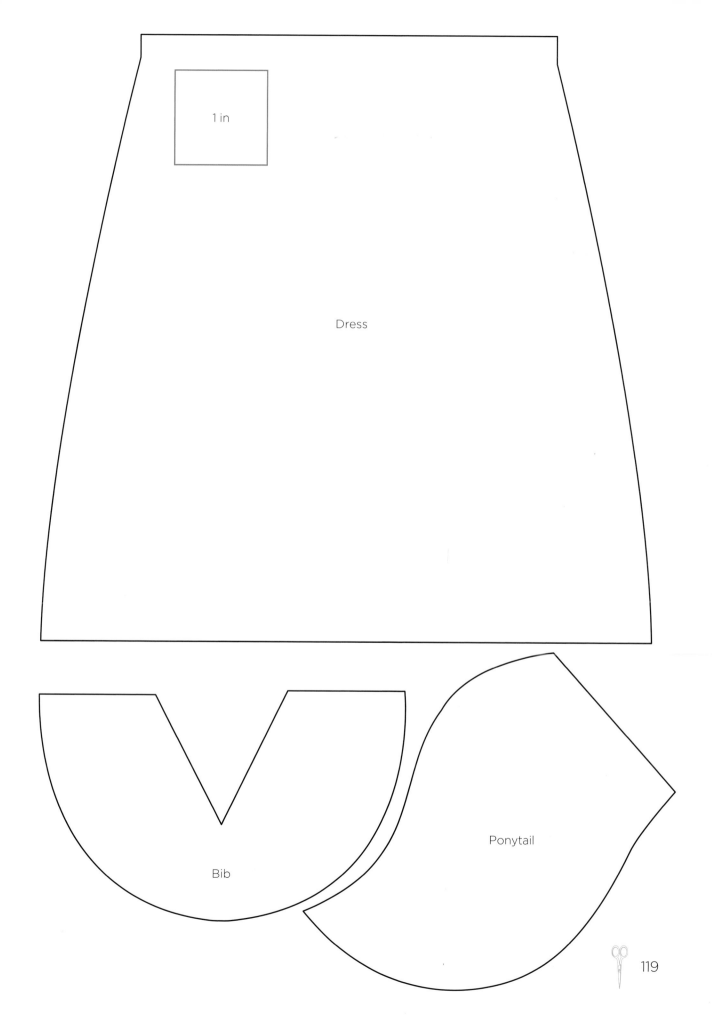

1 in

Dress

Bib

Ponytail

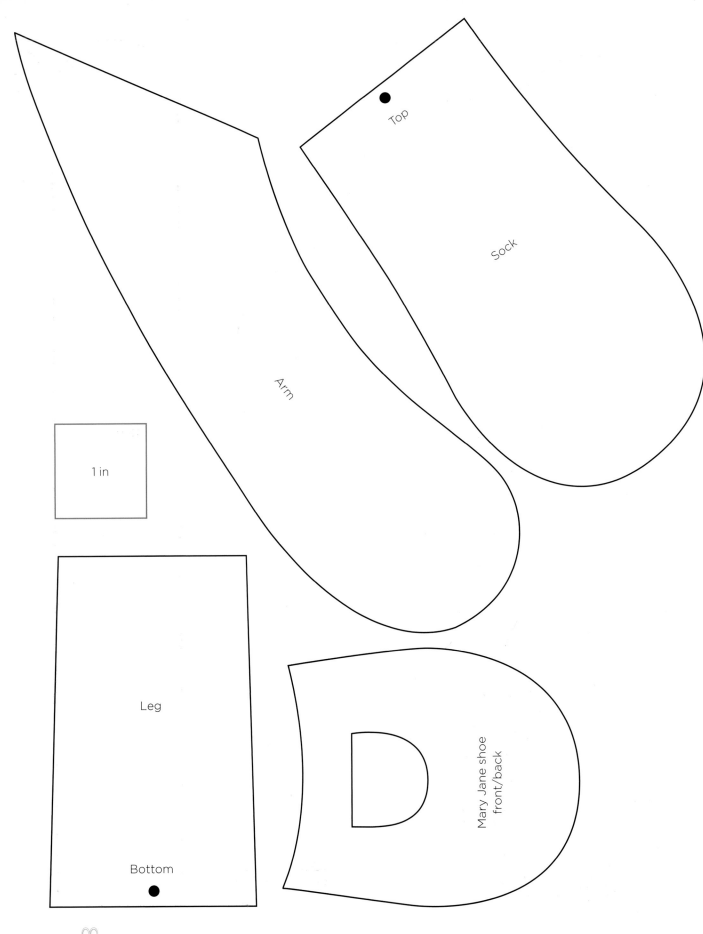

Top

Sock

Arm

1 in

Leg

Bottom

Mary Jane shoe
front/back

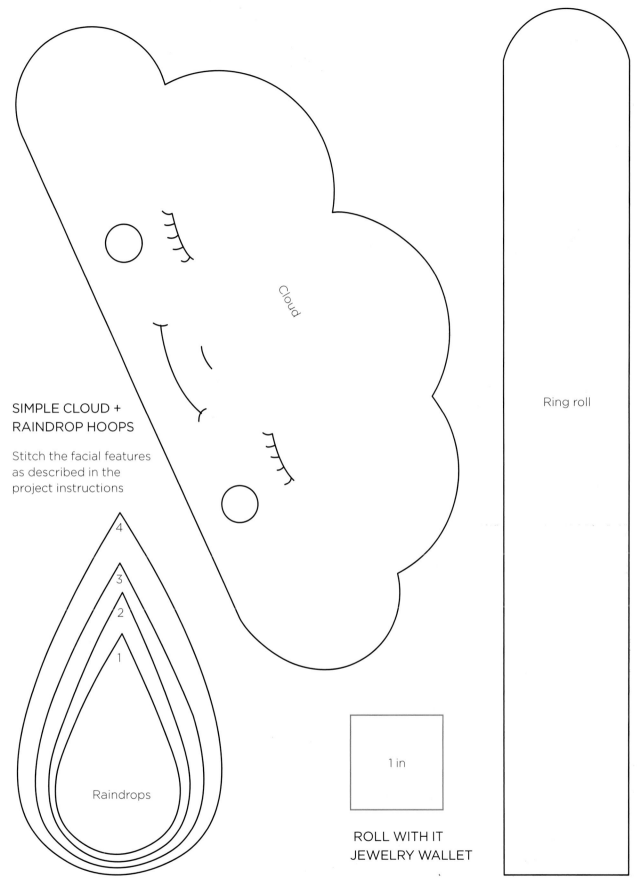

SIMPLE CLOUD +
RAINDROP HOOPS

Stitch the facial features
as described in the
project instructions

Cloud

4

3

2

1

Raindrops

Ring roll

1 in

ROLL WITH IT
JEWELRY WALLET

1 in

BRIGHT AS A BUTTON MAKE-UP POUCH

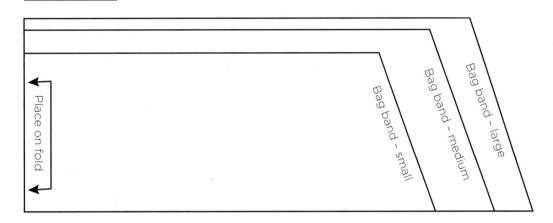

Place on fold

Bag band – small

Bag band – medium

Bag band – large

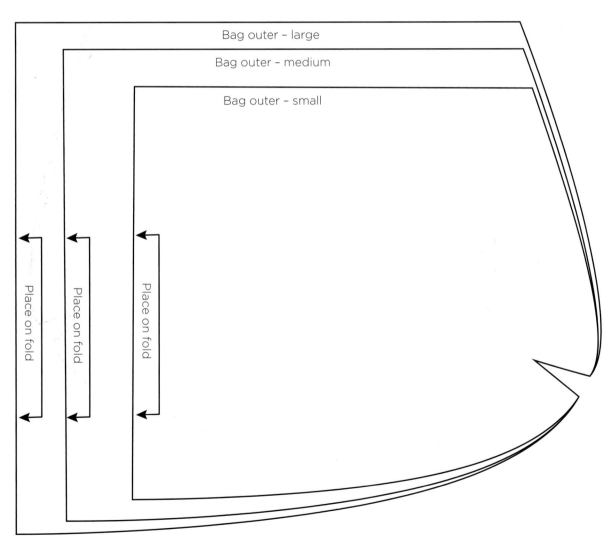

Bag outer – large

Bag outer – medium

Bag outer – small

Place on fold

Place on fold

Place on fold

1 in

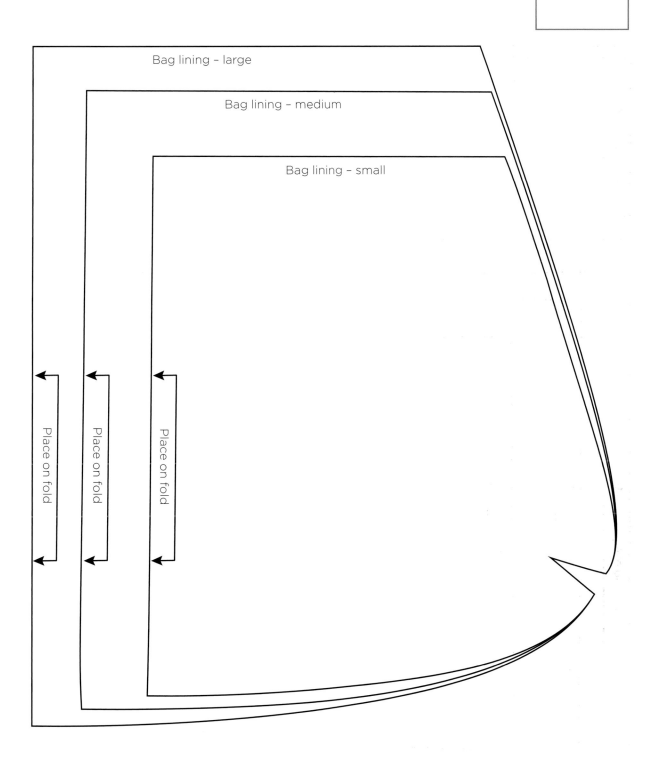

Bag lining – large

Bag lining – medium

Bag lining – small

Place on fold

Place on fold

Place on fold

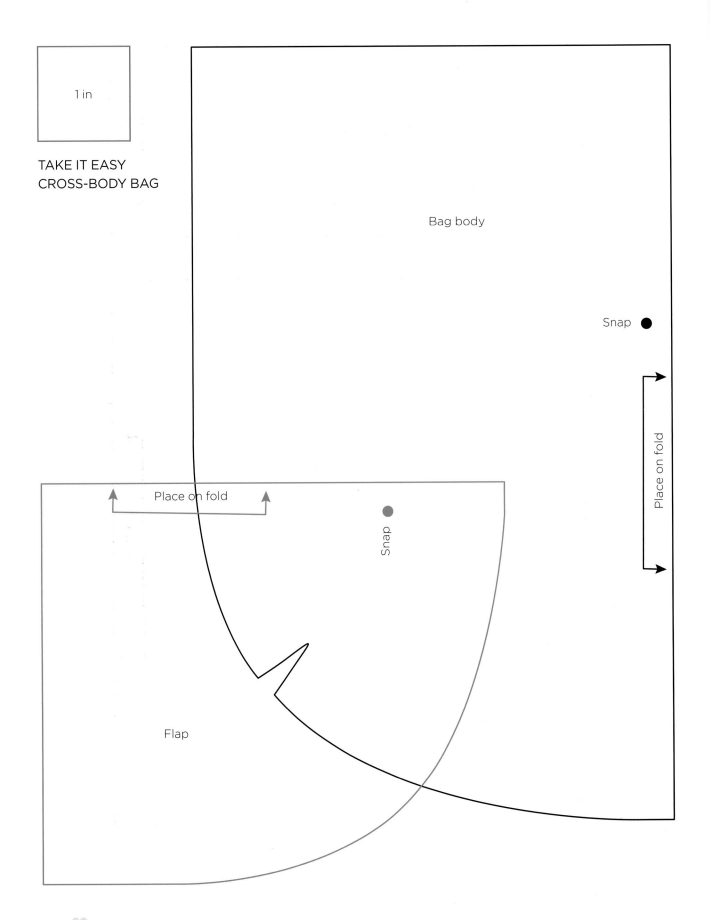

1 in

TAKE IT EASY
CROSS-BODY BAG

Bag body

Snap ●

Place on fold

Place on fold

Snap

Flap

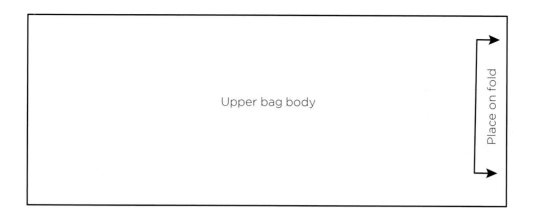

Upper bag body

Place on fold

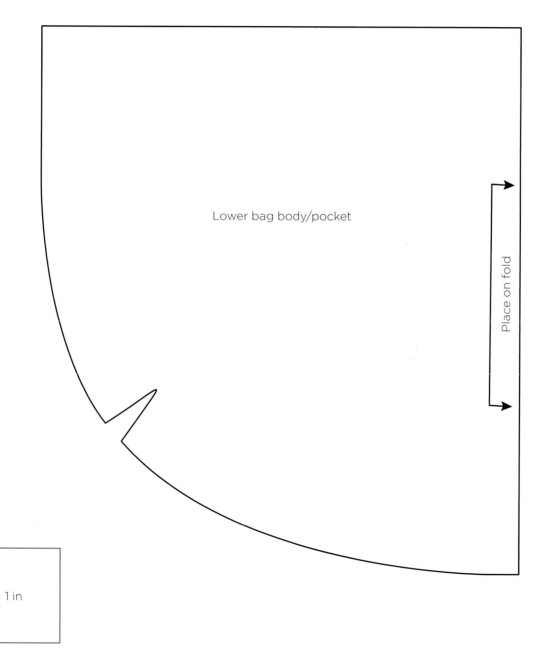

Lower bag body/pocket

Place on fold

1 in

RESOURCES

For basic sewing supplies, such as thread, needles, pins, quilting rulers, and fabric, try your local quilt or fabric shop. In the US, Jo-Ann Fabric and Craft Stores have a huge selection of everything you need to get started, as well as batting (wadding), stabilizers, interfacing, and fusible web. Below you will find a few of my favorite online sources for designer quilting cottons and sewing notions.

USA

www.fatquartershop.com
For cotton solids, new quilting cotton prints by the yard, and pre-cuts of all sizes

www.eQuilter.com
For an immense selection of quilting cotton prints

www.etsy.com
For quilting cottons and Essex linen – hundreds of fabric shops to choose from! Many of the fabrics from this book were found at the following shops: StashModernFabric, fabricsupply, IndeedFabric, sewmeasong, DonnasLavenderNest, and FreshModernFabric

www.etsy.com/shop/zipit
For high quality YKK zippers in numerous lengths and colors

www.etsy.com/shop/cowgirlsnaps
For gorgeous pearl no-sew snaps in many colors

UK & EUROPE

www.cotton-color.com
For quilting fabrics and sewing supplies

www.eternalmaker.co.uk
For quilting fabrics and sewing supplies

www.stitchcraftcreate.co.uk
For quilting fabrics and sewing supplies

www.thecottonpatch.co.uk
For quilting fabrics and sewing supplies

AUSTRALIA

www.patchwork-online.com.au
For quilting fabrics and sewing supplies

www.fabrictraders.com.au
For quilting fabrics and sewing supplies

www.hobbysew.com
For quilting fabrics and sewing supplies

ABOUT THE AUTHOR

Kim Kruzich is a designer, blogger, and teacher. She founded her business, Retro Mama, in 2006 and specializes in creating cheery, easy-to-stitch sewing patterns. She contributed projects to the book *Zakka Style* (C&T Publishing) and *Make It Yourself* magazine, and has been featured in *Mollie Makes*, *Crafts Beautiful*, and *Australian Homespun*. She has also authored several popular sewing tutorials on her blog. Kim and her husband Paul live in Indiana with their two sons and four rescue dogs. Follow or contact Kim at the following sites:

 www.retromama.com

 www.retro-mama.blogspot.com

 www.etsy.com/shop/retromama

 theretromama@gmail.com

ACKNOWLEDGMENTS

Thank you Paul, for always encouraging me to pursue my dreams, and thanks to all my family and friends; your enthusiasm, support, and love have made all of this possible. Also, thank you to everyone at F&W Media, especially Ame Verso for seeing my potential and for your guidance, Jennifer Stanley and Charlotte Andrew for helping to create this beautiful book, and Lin Clements for your patient and careful eye to fine tune my words. Many thanks to Jinger Schroeder, for your help and support through the years, and for your lovely idea that inspired the Fox Clothespin Bag. To all my online friends: I wouldn't be where I am without you. I cannot thank you enough for your positivity, excitement, and for welcoming me onto your computers and into your sewing rooms.

INDEX

A DAVID & CHARLES BOOK
© F&W Media International, Ltd 2015

David & Charles is an imprint of F&W Media International, Ltd
Brunel House, Forde Close, Newton Abbot, TQ12 4PU, UK

F&W Media International, Ltd is a subsidiary of F+W Media, Inc
10151 Carver Road, Suite #200, Blue Ash, OH 45242, USA

Text, Designs and Step Photography
© Kim Kruzich 2015
Layout and Styled Photography © F&W Media International, Ltd 2015

First published in the UK and USA in 2015

Kim Kruzich has asserted her right to be identified as author of this work in
accordance with the Copyright, Designs and Patents Act, 1988.

A catalogue record for this book is available from the British Library.

ISBN-13: 978-1-4463-0521-8 paperback
ISBN-10: 1-4463-0521-X paperback

ISBN-13: 978-1-4463-6943-2 PDF
ISBN-10: 1-4463-6943-9 PDF

ISBN-13: 978-1-4463-6942-5 EPUB
ISBN-10: 1-4463-6942-0 EPUB

Printed in China by RR Donnelley for:
F&W Media International, Ltd
Brunel House, Forde Close, Newton Abbot, TQ12 4PU, UK

10 9 8 7 6 5 4 3 2 1

Content Director: Ame Verso
Desk Editor: Charlotte Andrew
Project Editor: Lin Clements
Designer: Jennifer Stanley
Photographer: Jack Kirby
Senior Production Controller: Beverley Richardson

F+W Media publishes high quality books on a wide range of subjects.
For more great book ideas visit: **www.stitchcraftcreate.co.uk**

Layout of the digital edition of this book may vary depending on reader
hardware and display settings.